SEAS AND OCEANS

CROSSAN SCHOOL LIBRARY

Designer	Keith Newell
Editorial Planning	Clark Robinson Limited
Editors	Michael Flaherty
	Yvonne Ibazebo
Picture Researcher	Emma Krikler
Illustrator	Mike Saunders
Consultant	David Flint
	University Lecturer

© Aladdin Books Ltd 1992

First published in
the United States in 1992 by
Gloucester Press
95 Madison Avenue
New York, NY 10016

Library of Congress Cataloging-in-Publication Data

Clark, John Owen Edward.
　　Sea and oceans / John O.E. Clark.
　　　p.　　cm — (Hands on science)
　　Includes index.
　　Summary: Discusses the formation of the world's oceans, their various layers, currents and waves, marine life, and other related topics. Includes projects.
　　ISBN 0-531-17368-2
　　1. Oceans—Juvenile literature. [1. Ocean.] I. Title. II. Series.
　　GC21.5.C53　　1992
　　551.46—dc20　　　　92-1515　　CIP　　AC

All rights reserved

Printed in Belgium

HANDS·ON·SCIENCE

SEAS AND OCEANS

JOHN CLARK

GLOUCESTER PRESS
New York · London · Toronto · Sydney

CONTENTS

This book is all about the seas and oceans. The topics covered include how the oceans were formed millions of years ago, and how they are an important source of food and minerals. The book also tells you about the underwater landscape and the various plants and animals that live deep in the ocean depths. It explains how we can use the ocean's energy to generate electricity, and looks at ways in which the ocean is being polluted by mankind. There are "hands on" projects for you to do which use everyday items as equipment. There are also "did you know?" panels of information for added interest.

THE WATERY PLANET	6
LIFE IN THE OCEANS	8
LAYERS OF WATER	10
INTO THE DEEP	12
UNDERWATER LANDSCAPE	14
WATER IN MOTION	16
OCEAN CURRENTS	18
EXPLORING THE OCEAN FLOOR	20
MINERAL RICHES OF THE OCEANS	22
FOOD FROM THE SEA	24
ENERGY FROM THE OCEANS	26
THREATS TO THE OCEANS	28
EARLY BELIEFS	30
GLOSSARY	31
INDEX	32

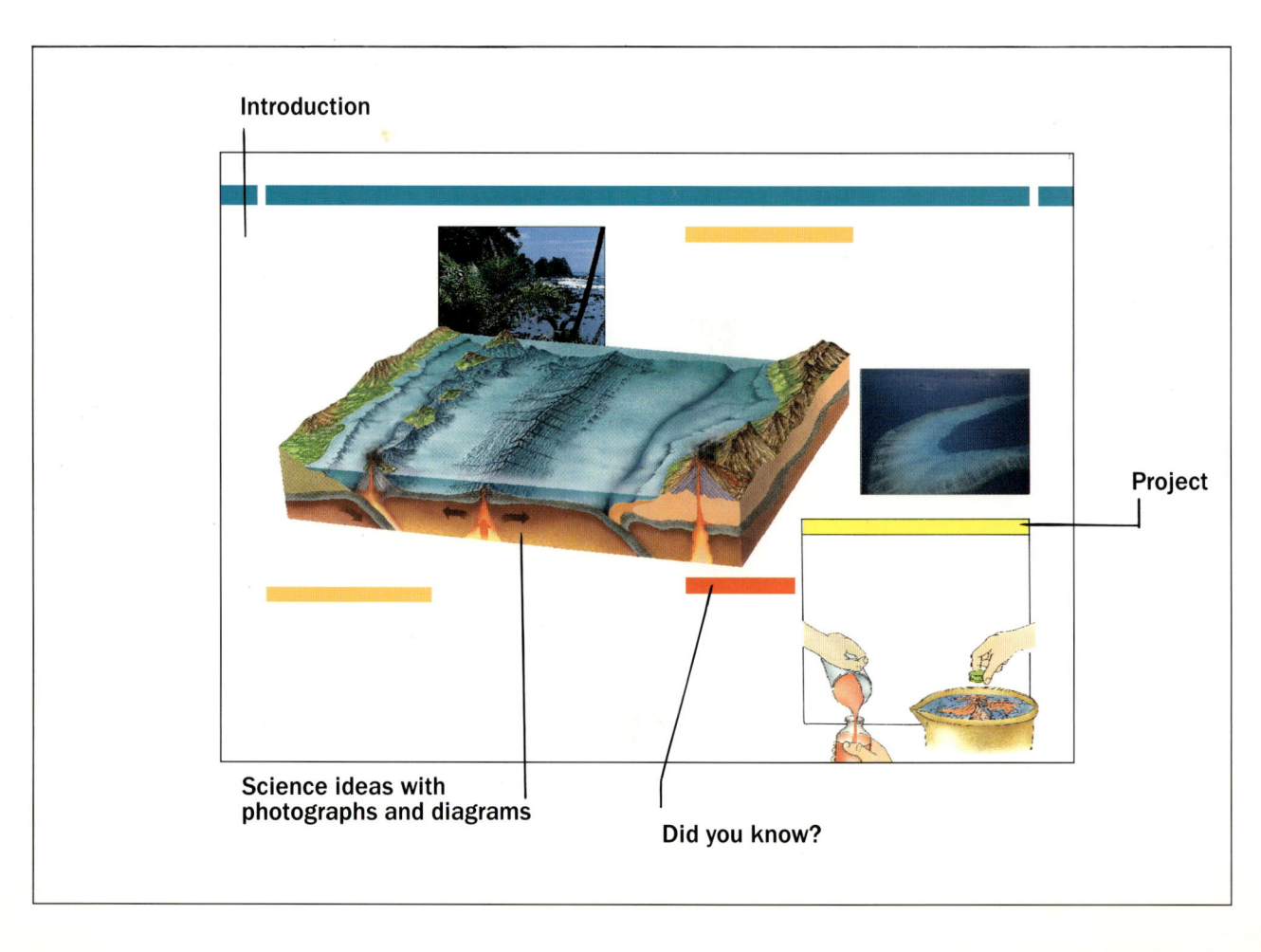

Introduction

Project

Science ideas with photographs and diagrams

Did you know?

INTRODUCTION

Seas and oceans cover nearly three-quarters of the earth's surface. Their waters are in constant motion because of powerful currents and tides. They are also home to thousands of different creatures, from shrimps and jellyfish to sharks and whales. The bottoms of the oceans are contoured by tall mountains, valleys and deep trenches. The seabed is also constantly changing as molten rock from beneath the earth's crust forces its way upward, and old rocks sink back into the mantle. Volcanoes situated underwater also erupt, and help to build new chains of islands.

Man has been interested in the seas and oceans for centuries. The early explorations used weighted rocks to measure the ocean depth, while today's modern vessels can plunge all the way to the seafloor and examine the landscape.

This book describes the origin, composition, and inhabitants of the oceans. It shows how the oceans can provide us with a rich source of food, mineral resources, and energy. The book also explains how pollution and other activities of mankind may be putting these natural resources at risk.

▽ Waves crashing into a huge rock in northern California's Pacific Ocean

6 THE WATERY PLANET

Most of the earth's surface is covered by the seas and oceans. This vast area of water — about 139 million square miles — surrounds the continents. When it is viewed from space, earth appears as a blue planet with the continents appearing as occasional islands of brown land.

FORMATION

The earth has not always been covered with water, and neither have the oceans always had their present shape. When the earth first formed, it was a fiery ball of hot rock dotted with thousands of active volcanoes. As the volcanoes erupted, they emitted gases, mainly water vapor and carbon dioxide, into the atmosphere. In time, the atmosphere became saturated with vapor and as the earth cooled, it condensed and fell as rain. The volcanoes produced more and more steam, and so the cycle continued. Over millions of years, the rainwater accumulated on the surface, forming the seas and oceans of today.

During this early period, much of the land was joined together like a huge island. Then the continents separated and drifted to their present positions.

▽ Oceans on earth began as steam from volcanoes, which condensed into rain clouds in the atmosphere. This rain gradually collected to form the world's oceans.

Water vapor and carbon dioxide

Forming atmosphere and oceans

Oceans

200 million yrs ago   100 million yrs ago   50 million yrs ago

SEAWATER

The oceans still get much of their water from rain. But the water does not just stay in the oceans, it is recycled. The sun heats up the oceans and makes the water evaporate into the atmosphere as water vapor. As the vapor cools, it forms clouds which eventually release rain back to the earth. The rain flows along rivers back into the sea.

The seawater also helps to regulate temperatures on land. The sea does not lose the sun's heat as fast as the land does. So during the cold winter months, breezes from the sea carry warm air to the land.

River water also washes various minerals into the sea. The most important one is salt (sodium chloride), which makes up an average of 3.5 percent by weight of seawater. Other minerals in seawater include sulfates, magnesium, potassium and calcium; there are even small traces of gold in the sea. Seawater also contains dissolved oxygen, which is essential for the life of fish and other marine animals and plants.

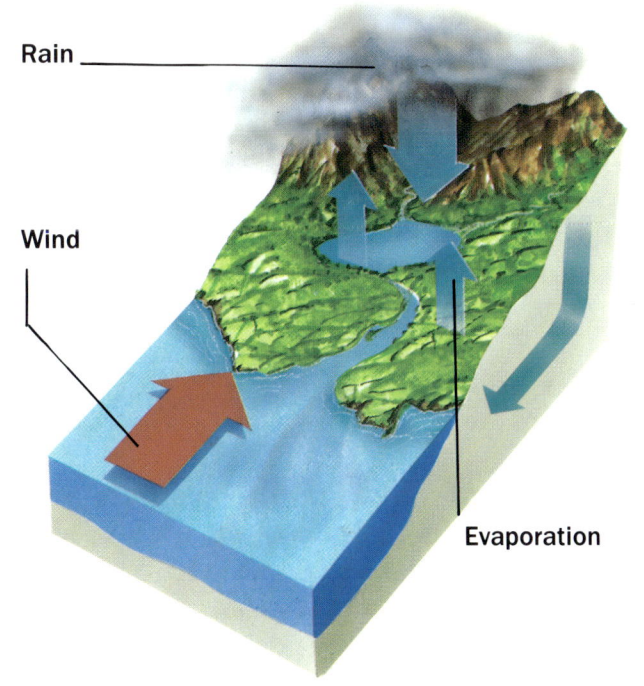

△ The water cycle circulates water on earth. Water evaporates from the oceans and forms clouds, which produce rain over the land.

▽ Water makes up 96.5 percent of the sea. The rest consists of dissolved minerals, the most important being common salt.

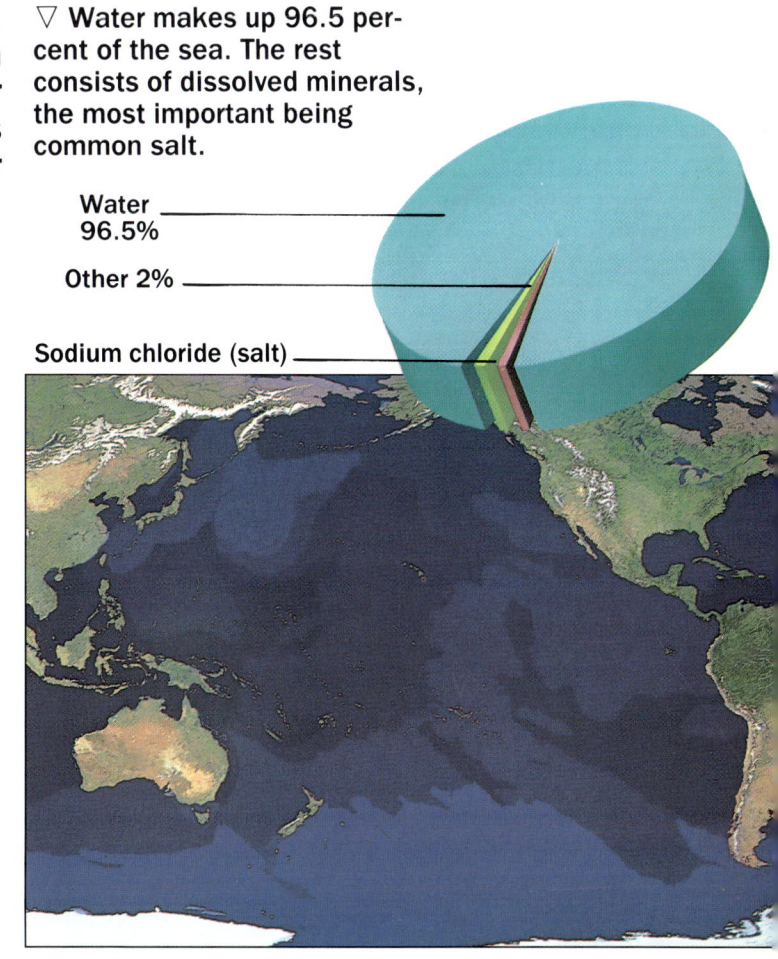

▽ The world's oceans changed in size and shape as the continents slowly drifted apart. The Atlantic Ocean gets 1 inch wider every year.

Present day

A satellite image of the Pacific Ocean

8 LIFE IN THE OCEANS

The oceans cover over 70 percent of the earth's surface, and have an average depth of 12,000 feet. Their waters therefore provide the largest available space for living things. All marine plant life, and most animals, live in fairly shallow waters near the surface. But even the ocean depths have some life.

EVOLUTION

Life on earth began in the ocean fringes. The sea consisted of a "soup" of biochemicals which combined on rocks at the shore to form the first living cells. The first single-celled animals lived in the sea. These gradually evolved into multi-celled creatures without backbones, resembling the shellfish, worms, and corals that live in the sea today.

Meanwhile, the green plants that had evolved on land helped to add oxygen to the earth's atmosphere. The oxygen that dissolved in seawater became available to marine animals. The first animals to evolve with backbones were fishlike creatures called placoderms, whose bodies were covered in bony plates. These were also the ancestors of amphibians, the first backboned animals to move onto dry land. Fish continued to evolve in the sea, eventually giving rise to sharklike predators with skeletons made of cartilage, and modern bony fish.

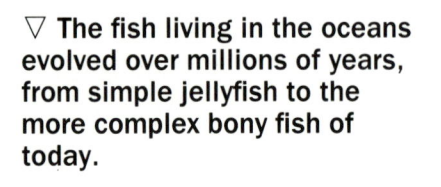

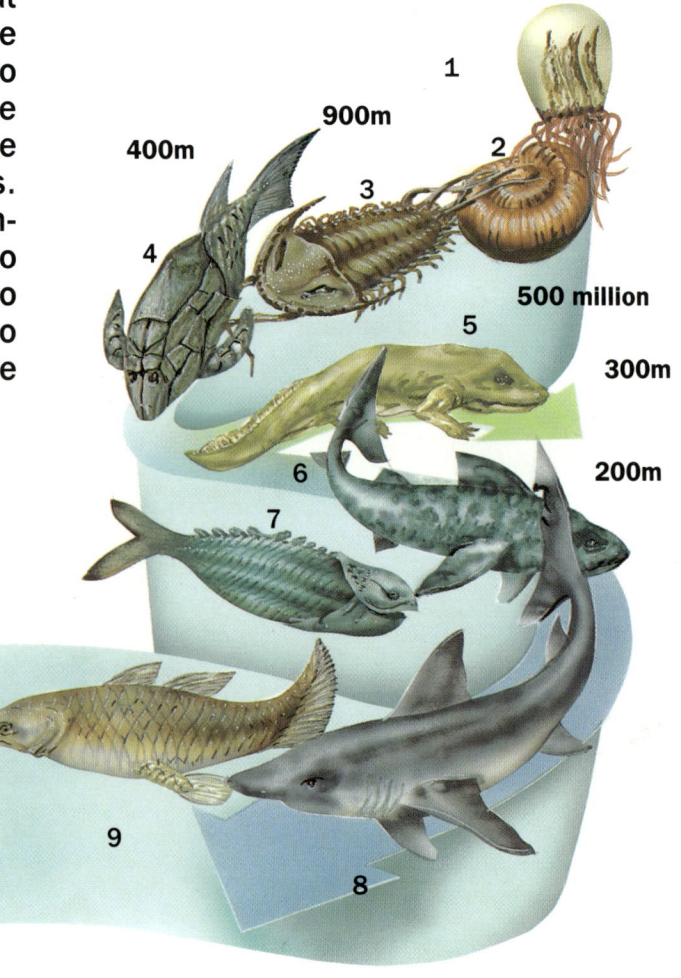

▽ The fish living in the oceans evolved over millions of years, from simple jellyfish to the more complex bony fish of today.

Coelacanth: a fish that dates back 300 million years.

(1) Jellyfish (2) Mollusk
(3) Trilobite (4) Placoderm
(5) Rachitomes (6) First shark
(7) Birkenia (8) Modern shark
(9) Holostean (10) Modern fish

Present day fish

LIVING IN WATER

Fish come in all shapes and sizes, from the small coral fish and sardines to the long, snakelike eels and huge basking sharks. And they have evolved various unique features to suit their life in the water. Fish have fins which they use to swim, and most have internal swim bladders that enable them to float in the water without sinking or rising to the surface. Cartilaginous fish such as the shark (right), have no swim bladders and sink if they stop swimming. All fish have gills which they use to extract oxygen dissolved in the sea. This allows them to "breathe" under the water.

Fast-swimming fish have streamlined bodies that move easily through the water. For example, a 6-ft long barracuda can swim at a speed of 40 feet a second (27 mph) and turn in its own body length.

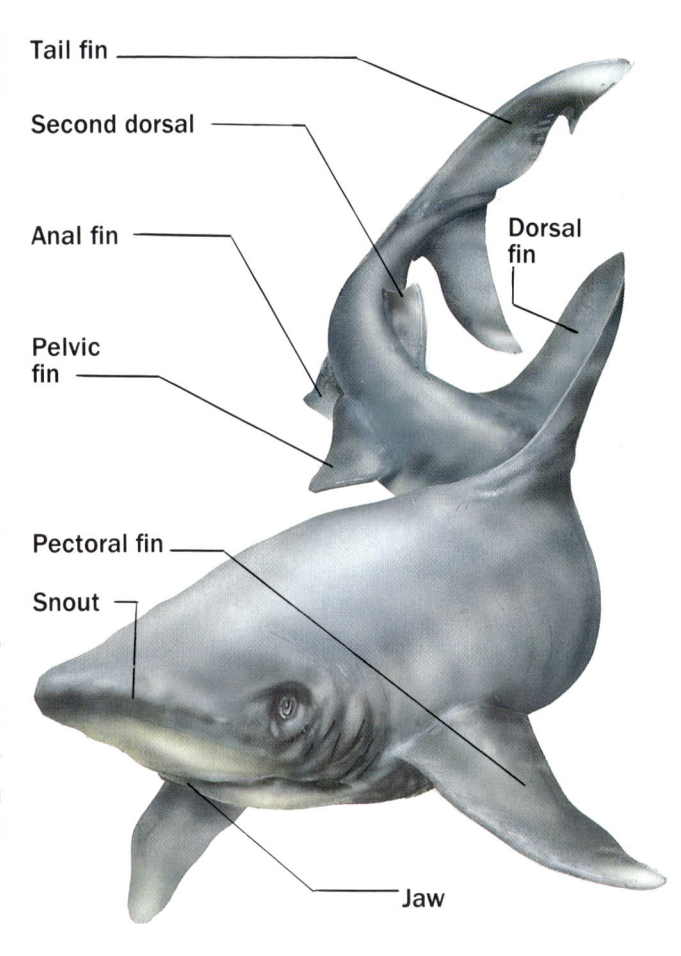

▽ Bony fish keep afloat by means of a swim bladder or air bladder. It is an elongated sac which contains air and lies above the digestive tract. The fish controls buoyancy by varying the amount and pressure of the air.

MAKE A SWIM BLADDER

You can see how a fish's swim bladder works by making a model from a small bottle with a tight-fitting top. Fill a large bowl with water, half-fill the bottle as well and screw on the top. Put the bottle in the bowl and see how it floats on the surface. Now gradually add more water to the bottle, screwing on the top and making it float each time. Eventually you will add the right amount of water for the bottle to just break the surface.

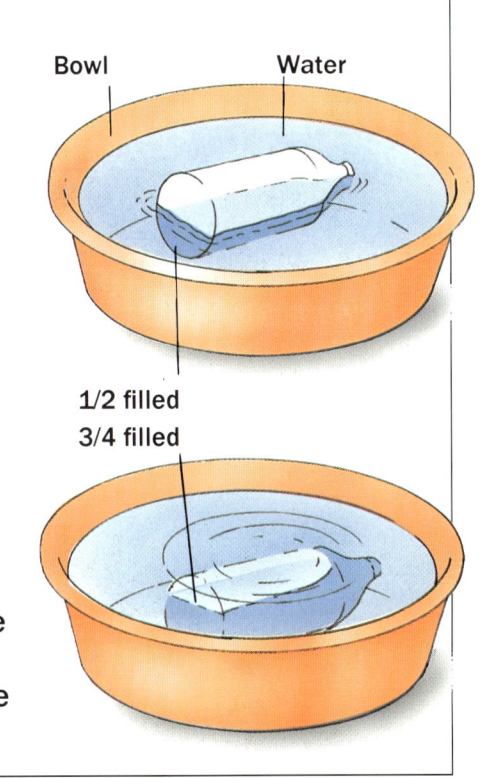

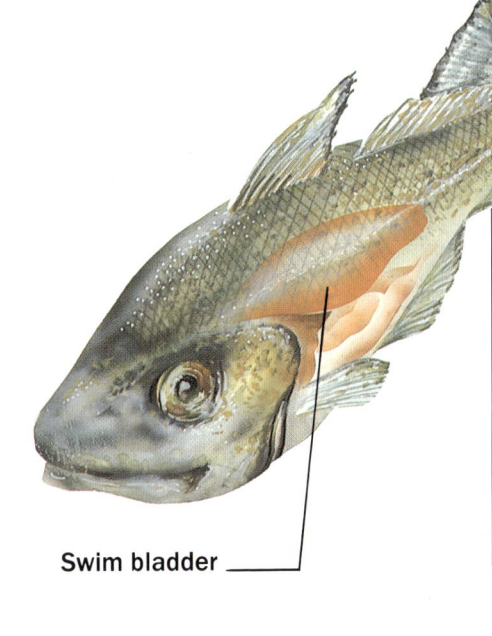

LAYERS OF WATER

Each type of life form in the sea is found at a particular depth, from the shallow areas a few feet deep to the abyssal plain more than 13,000 feet deep. The amount of sunlight and the saltiness of the water also determines the kind of plants and animals that are found at each ocean level.

THE CONTINENTAL SHELF

The continental shelf is the shallowest part of the sea. It starts at the edge of the continents and gently slopes downward. The shelf is seldom more than 500 feet deep, and is also known as the euphotic zone. Because sunlight reaches the bottom of the shelf, seaweed grows in this layer. The tiny animals near the surface, which are called zooplankton, consist of krill and other small shrimplike crustaceans, as well as the eggs and young of various fish.

Apart from eating microscopic plants called phytoplankton, krill are a source of food for a range of marine creatures, from surface-feeding fish to baleen whales. Jellyfish also live near the surface, drifting with the currents and using the stinging cells in their tentacles to trap and kill small fish for food.

▽ The sea depth changes as you move away from land. Nearest the shore the sea is quite shallow. It tends to be deeper further out.

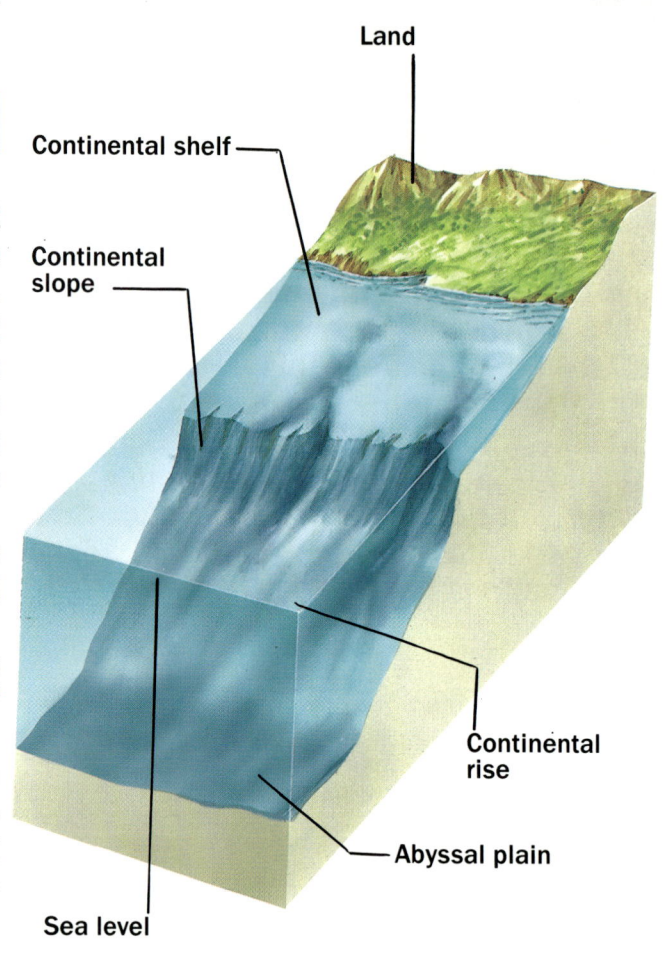

Land
Continental shelf
Continental slope
Continental rise
Abyssal plain
Sea level

Continental shelves extend around the edges of continents

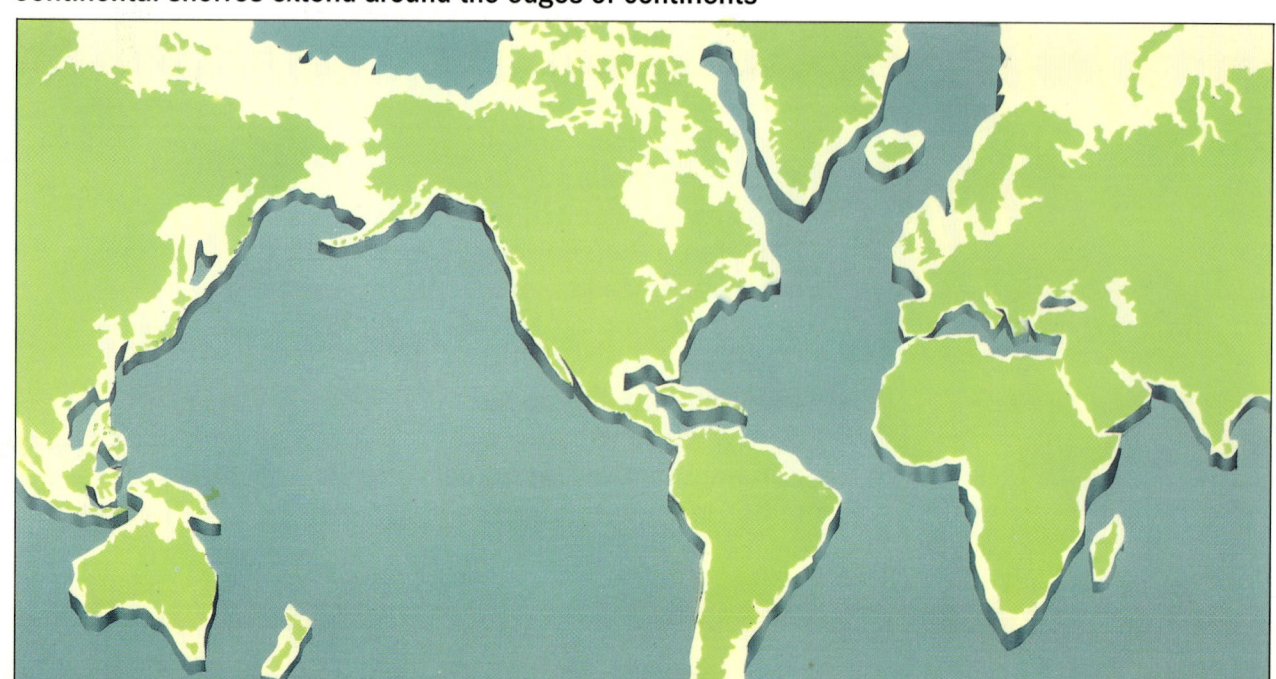

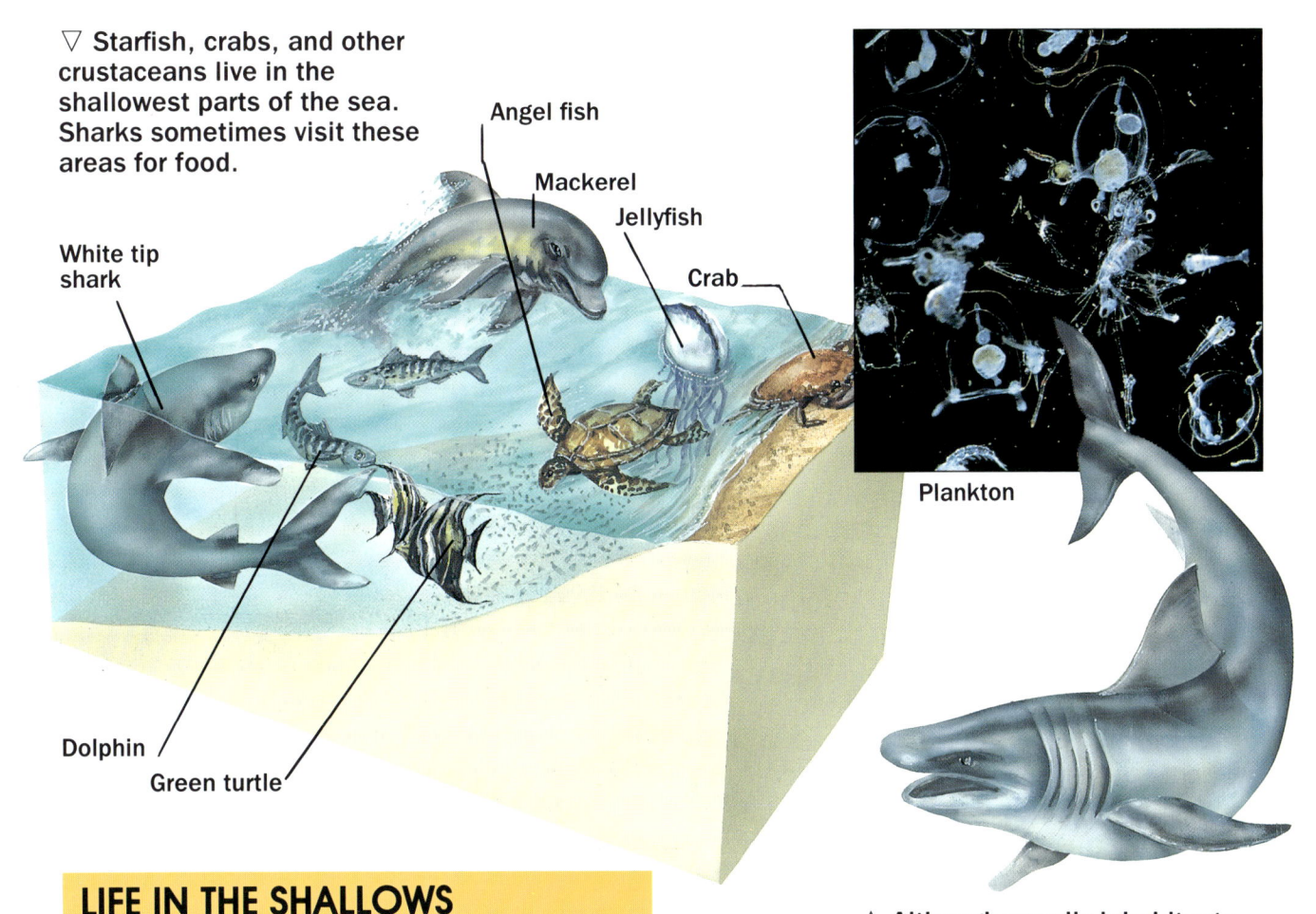

▽ Starfish, crabs, and other crustaceans live in the shallowest parts of the sea. Sharks sometimes visit these areas for food.

White tip shark
Angel fish
Mackerel
Jellyfish
Crab
Dolphin
Green turtle
Plankton

△ Although usually inhabitants of deeper water, white sharks swim into shallow water to feed. The large whale shark however, feeds only on plankton.

LIFE IN THE SHALLOWS

Most fish live in the shallow parts of the oceans, and end up feeding on each other. Small fish swim in shoals for protection, while predators such as barracuda and sharks swoop in to catch their prey. Other fish, such as conger eels, wait in rock crevices for their prey to swim within range. Flatfish scavenge on the bottom, quickly burying themselves in the sand or even changing color when danger threatens.

Most of the predatory fish are active during the day. So at night, when it is less dangerous, other fish leave the deeper layers and swim upward to feed in the shallows. Some of the plankton which live near the surface give off light, and so it is never completely dark, even at night. This light helps the night feeders to find food more easily.

Some inland lakes, such as the Caspian Sea and the Dead Sea, are so salty that they resemble shallow seas.

Salt crystals in the Dead Sea area

12 INTO THE DEEP

The layer of ocean water lying beyond the shallow surface is called the mesopelagic zone. It has a depth of about 6,000 feet. The bathypelagic is the next layer and it reaches all the way to the bottom, or ocean plain, with a depth of about 13,200 feet. No light penetrates either of these layers.

THE OCEAN PLAIN

The ocean plain is not a wide, flat area, but consists of tall mountain ranges, canyons, and gorges. Mountains over 10,000 feet tall are common. Some of them were formed by mountain-building processes and erosion on land before becoming submerged under the sea. Others have been carved out by underwater currents. Sloping canyons are carved from turbid currents — resembling underwater avalanches — which sweep mud and sand further out to sea. Rivers wash silt and other sediment out to sea, and this settles at the bottom of oceans.

The continents and ocean basins "ride" on huge slabs of the earth's crust, called plates. Where the edge of one ocean plate slips under another plate, a deep trench forms. Some of the trenches drop down for more than six miles. The Challenger deep in the Pacific Ocean's Marianas Trench, for example, is over 36,000 feet deep.

A computer-generated map of the ocean depths

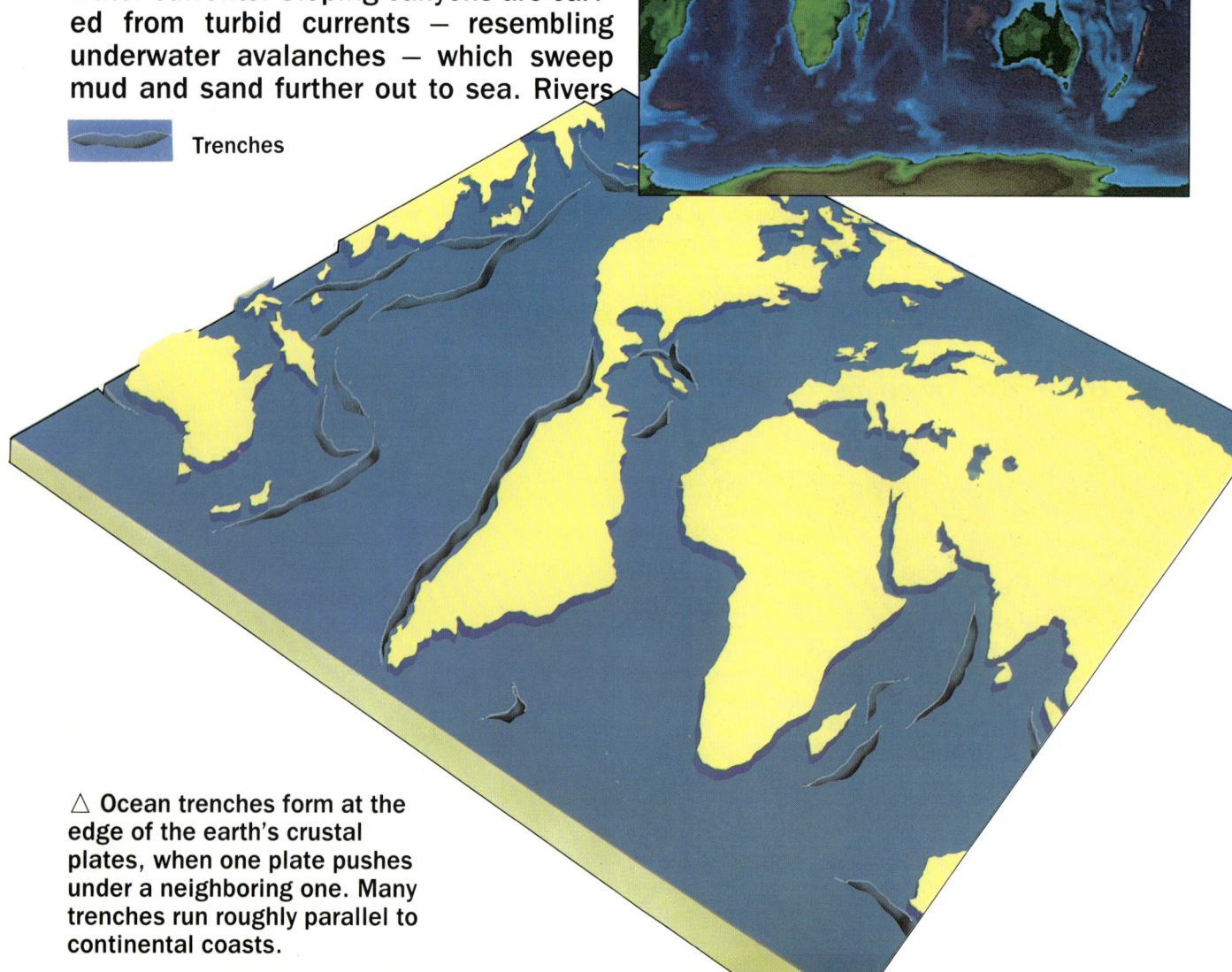

Trenches

△ Ocean trenches form at the edge of the earth's crustal plates, when one plate pushes under a neighboring one. Many trenches run roughly parallel to continental coasts.

GOING DOWN

Many factors change with increasing depth in the oceans. Sunlight is only able to penetrate to a depth of about 300 feet, and this area is known as the photic zone. By a depth of about 3,000 feet, there is a twilight zone where visibility is reduced to a few yards. No light reaches the bathypelagic zone.

The temperature of the oceans falls with increasing depth. Near the surface, temperature depends mainly on the climate, and it is hotter in the tropics than at the poles. Evaporation and the inflow of river water also affects the surface temperatures. By a depth of about 6,500 feet however, the temperature falls to about 37°F and remains more or less constant. This is because there are few deep currents at this level to mix the water.

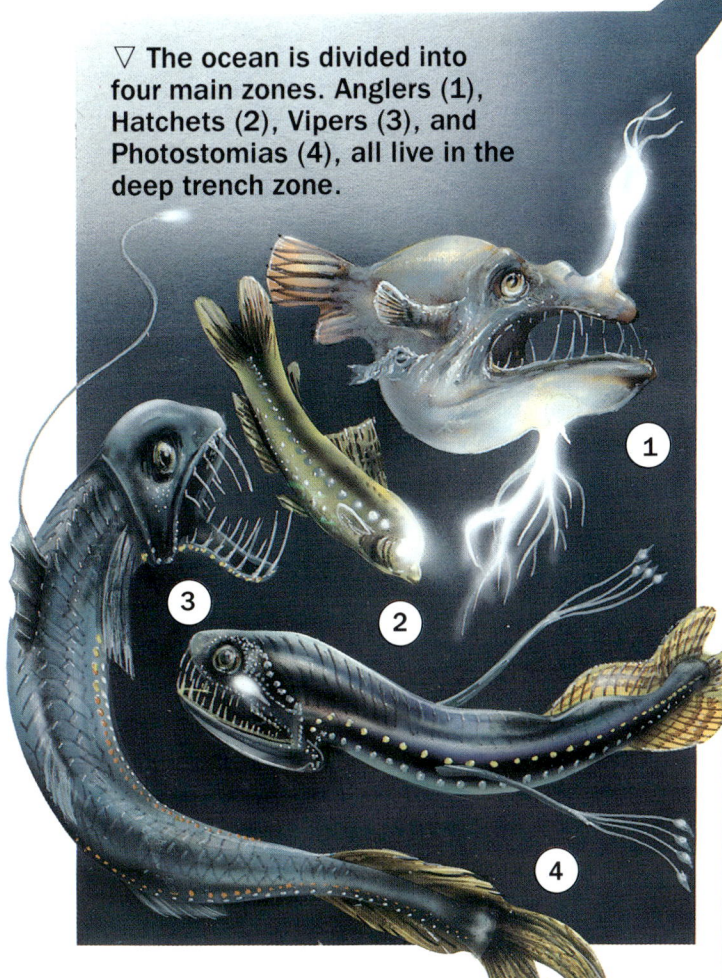

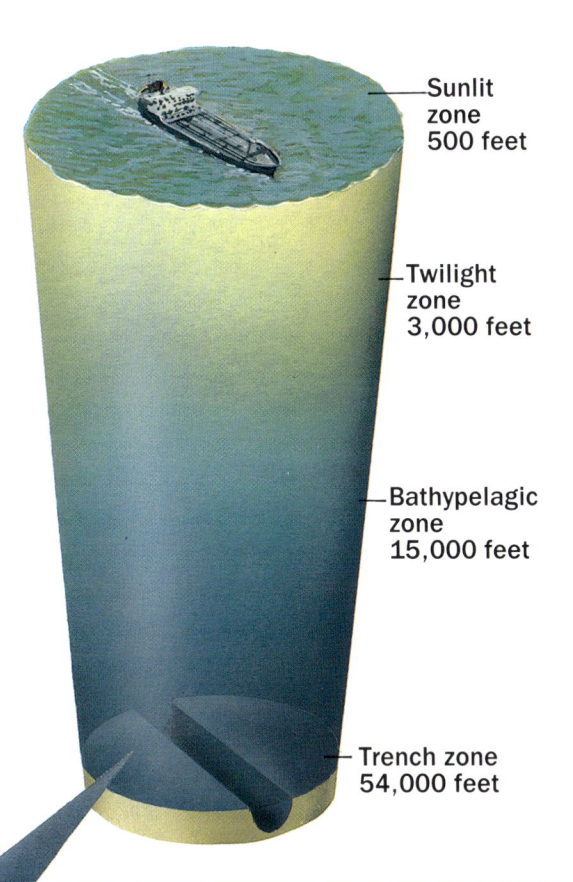

- Sunlit zone 500 feet
- Twilight zone 3,000 feet
- Bathypelagic zone 15,000 feet
- Trench zone 54,000 feet

▽ The ocean is divided into four main zones. Anglers (1), Hatchets (2), Vipers (3), and Photostomias (4), all live in the deep trench zone.

DEEPSEA LIFE

Fish that live in deep water feed mainly on the remains of dead surface animals that sink to the bottom. Some strange fish inhabit the inky blackness of the deepest oceans. Many of them have large mouths which they always keep open as they swim around, looking for prey. Others have luminous spots of light which enable them recognize each other and their neighbors. The various angler fish have a luminous blob at the end of a projection from their heads, which acts as a lure to tempt prey within reach.

A deep-sea fish underwater

14 UNDERWATER LANDSCAPE

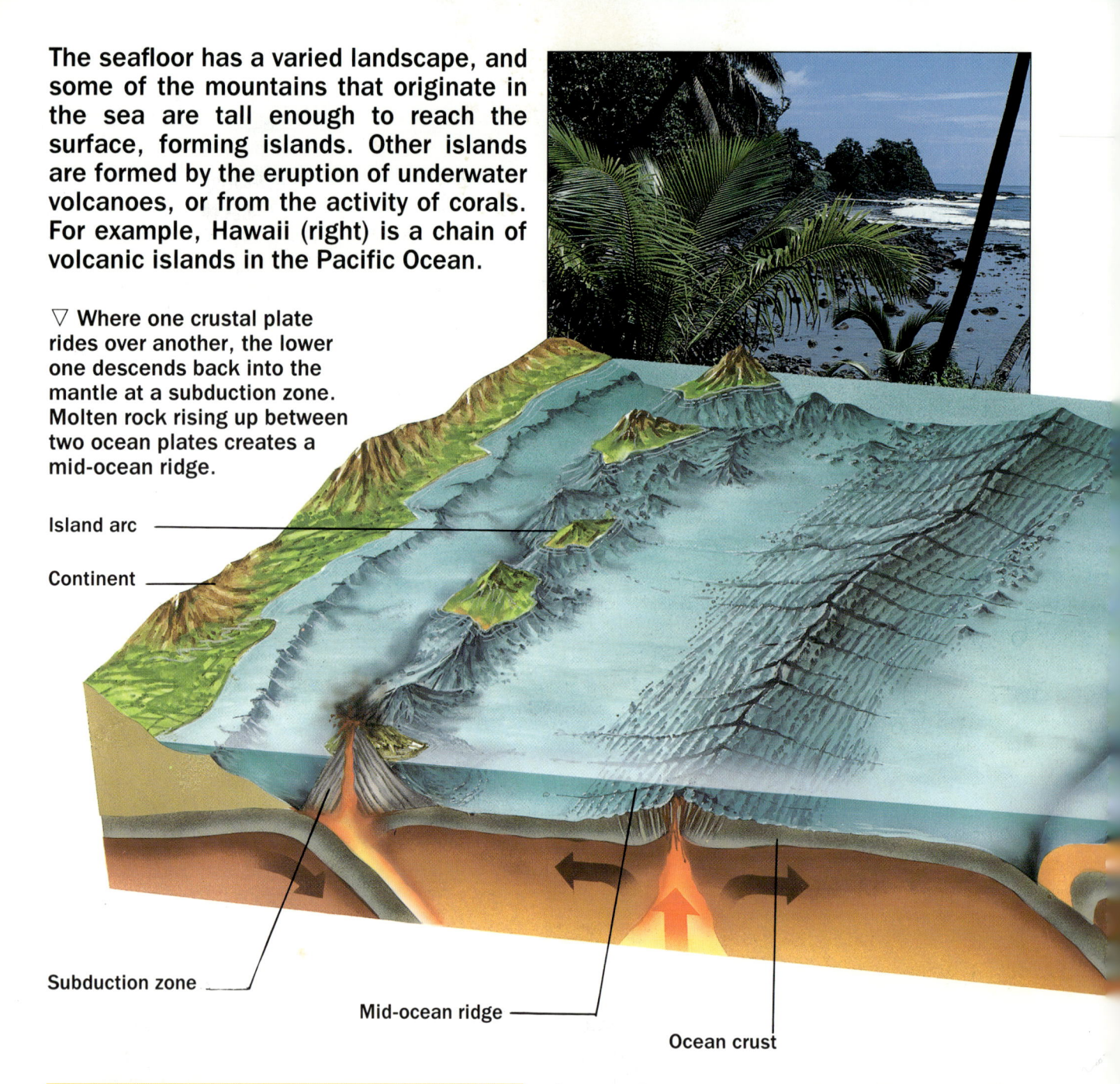

The seafloor has a varied landscape, and some of the mountains that originate in the sea are tall enough to reach the surface, forming islands. Other islands are formed by the eruption of underwater volcanoes, or from the activity of corals. For example, Hawaii (right) is a chain of volcanic islands in the Pacific Ocean.

▽ Where one crustal plate rides over another, the lower one descends back into the mantle at a subduction zone. Molten rock rising up between two ocean plates creates a mid-ocean ridge.

Island arc
Continent
Subduction zone
Mid-ocean ridge
Ocean crust

MID-OCEAN RIDGES

Down the center of the major oceans, the crustal plates are gradually moving apart. This happens because molten rock from the earth's mantle constantly wells up between them. As this hot lava cools, it forms a pair of parallel ridges. These are known as mid-ocean ridges. The whole process is called seafloor spreading, and it causes the plates of the oceans and continents to gradually move apart. The rocks in the ridges are the youngest in the earth's crust. The Mid-Atlantic Ridge, for example, runs southward from Iceland along the center of the Atlantic Ocean, until it curves eastward to join the Indian Ocean Ridge.

In some places, volcanoes rise up to 3,000 feet from the seabed to form tall, underwater mountains. In shallower parts of the ocean, the volcanoes may even be tall enough to break the surface as islands. Waves may wear away the top of a volcanic island, and such submerged islands are called flat-topped guyots, or seamounts.

REEF FORMATION

Corals are small animals related to jellyfish and sea anemones. They extract a chalky substance, calcium carbonate, from seawater and use it to build their skeletons. When the corals die, their skeletons remain as gnarled rocky growths. Corals live only in well-lit, warm tropical waters no deeper than 180 feet. Near a shore, corals build up to form a fringing reef; further out they form a barrier reef.

Sometimes corals form a fringing reef around a volcanic island. As the volcanic peak is eroded and the sea level rises, the coral continues to grow toward the shallows. Finally the island sinks, leaving a ring of coral known as an atoll. This explains why such islands have deep, clifflike sides of coral when viewed from underwater.

Trench

Volcano

The Great Barrier Reef of Australia

DID YOU KNOW?

A coral reef is a self-contained habitat for many organisms. The Great Barrier Reef in Australia, for example, is home to over 3,000 different species. In addition to fish, there are crabs, jellyfish, sea anemones, sea cucumbers (which are animals), and starfish. Even the corals themselves are animals.

MAKE AN UNDERWATER VOLCANO

You can mimic the effect of an underwater volcano. Pour cold water into a bucket until it is nearly full. Then fill a small plastic bottle with hot water, adding a few drops of colored dye. Screw the cap on the bottle and place it at the bottom of the bucket. Now unscrew the cap and watch as the less dense hot water rises to the surface.

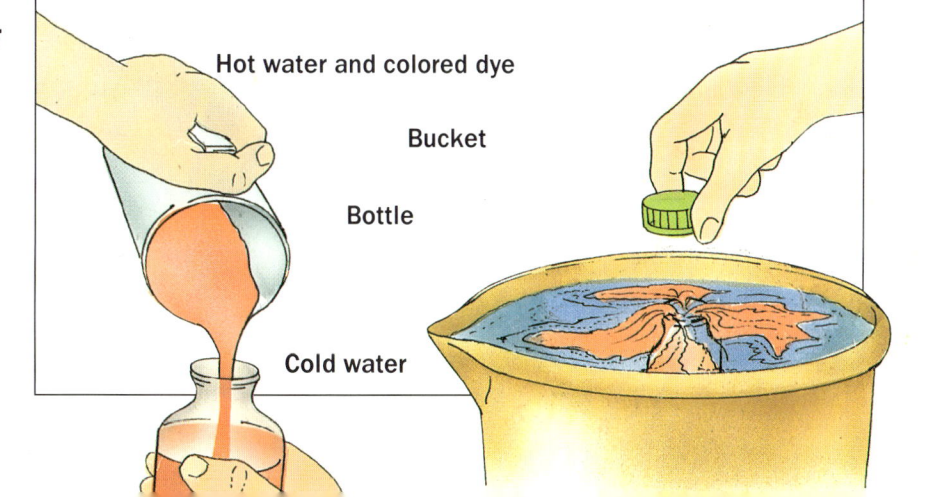

Hot water and colored dye

Bucket

Bottle

Cold water

16 WATER IN MOTION

The water in the oceans is constantly on the move. At the surface, wind whips the sea up into waves that move over great distances. The gravitational pull of the moon and sun also causes tides to rise and fall each day. In addition to all these movements, underwater currents shift masses of water around the world.

WAVE MOVEMENT

Waves are caused by an up-and-down movement of water — only when waves break on the shore do they make water move along. The waves are merely large versions of the ripples you see on ponds. You can demonstrate their movement by making a cork float in a pond and dropping a stone into the water near it. As the ripples pass the cork, they make it bob up and down in the same place.

In the open sea, wind starts wave movement. Particles of water circulate immediately under the waves, and at the surface this movement may cause a wave to break, or turn over. Waves can travel over great distances and the distance between wave peaks is known as the wavelength.

Waves that reach the shore change the landscape. They form beaches, erode cliffs and gradually alter shorelines. Waves also carry beach sand away with them into the oceans.

△ Cliffs, such as these at Marsden Bay in England, are eroded by the action of waves.

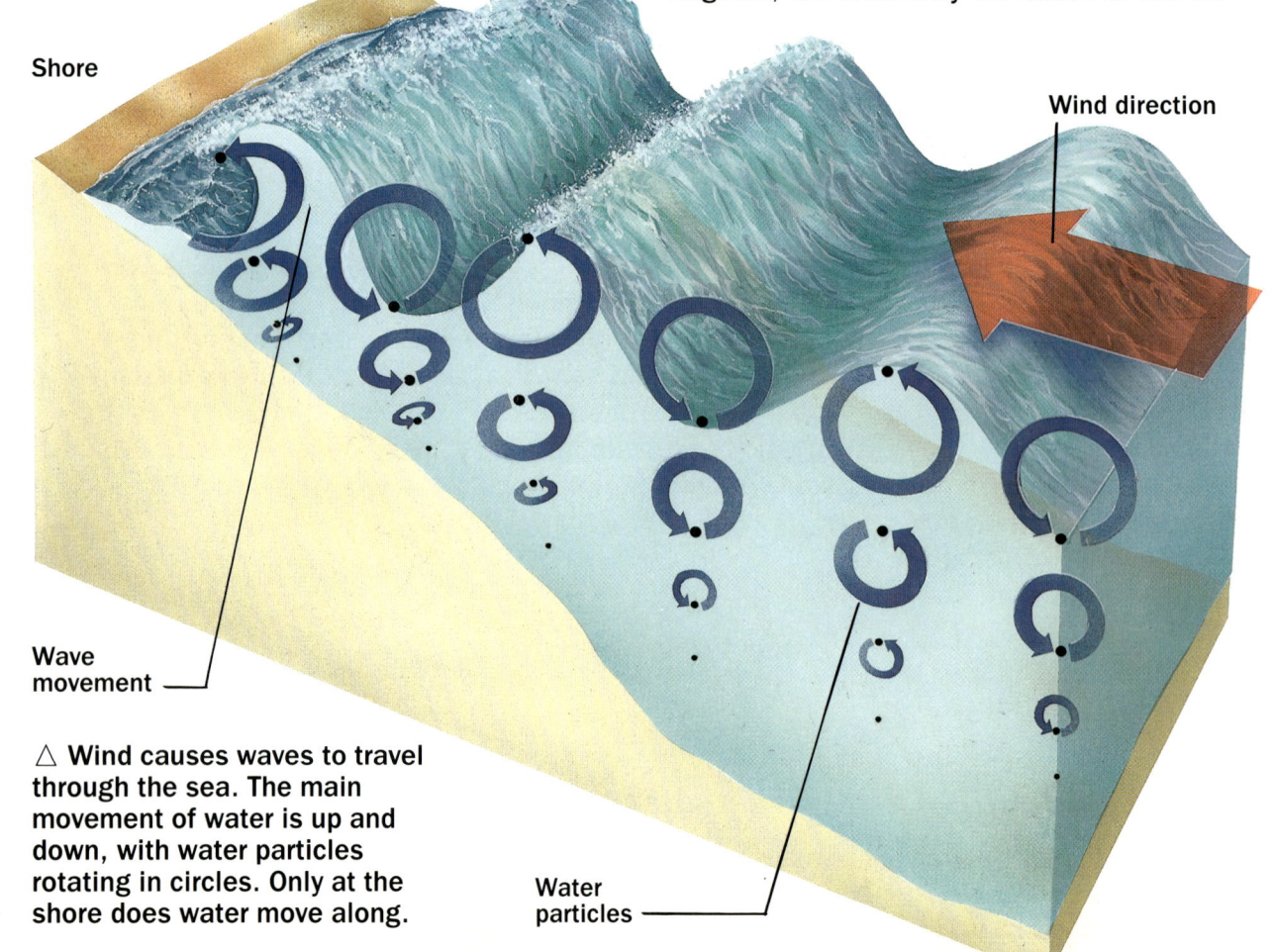

△ Wind causes waves to travel through the sea. The main movement of water is up and down, with water particles rotating in circles. Only at the shore does water move along.

TIDES

The gravitational attraction of the moon pulls the waters of the ocean into a bulge, or high tide, when the moon is directly overhead. Because the earth rotates on its axis, centrifugal forces acting on the water cause a similar bulge on the opposite side. The sun's gravity also affects the oceans and the combined effect of all these forces causes the bulge of water to move around the earth, making the sea level rise and fall as tides.

A different effect called a tidal wave is caused by underwater earthquakes. Tidal waves have very long wavelengths and travel at hundreds of miles per hour. As they approach the shore, their height increases to several feet.

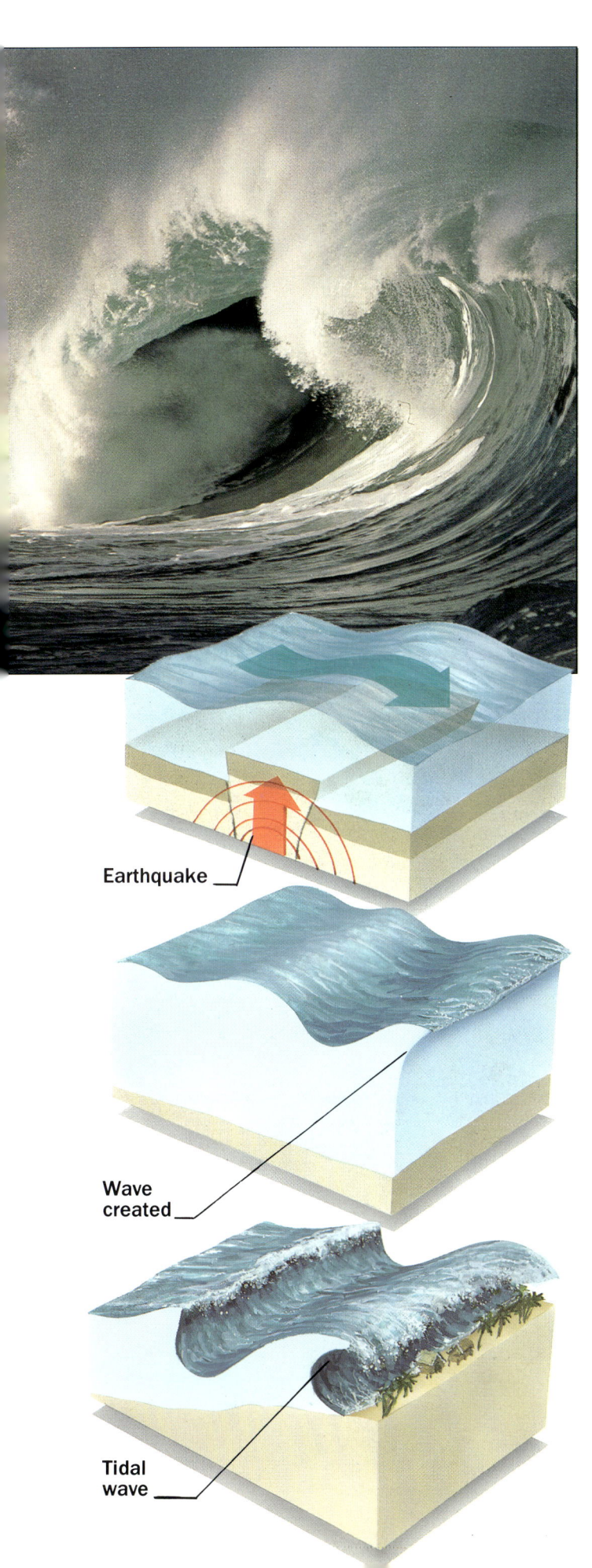

Spring tide
New moon
Sun

Leap tide
Half moon
Sun

⇨ Gravitational pull of sun
⇨ Gravitational pull of moon
▬ Solar tide
▬ Lunar tide

Earthquake
Wave created
Tidal wave

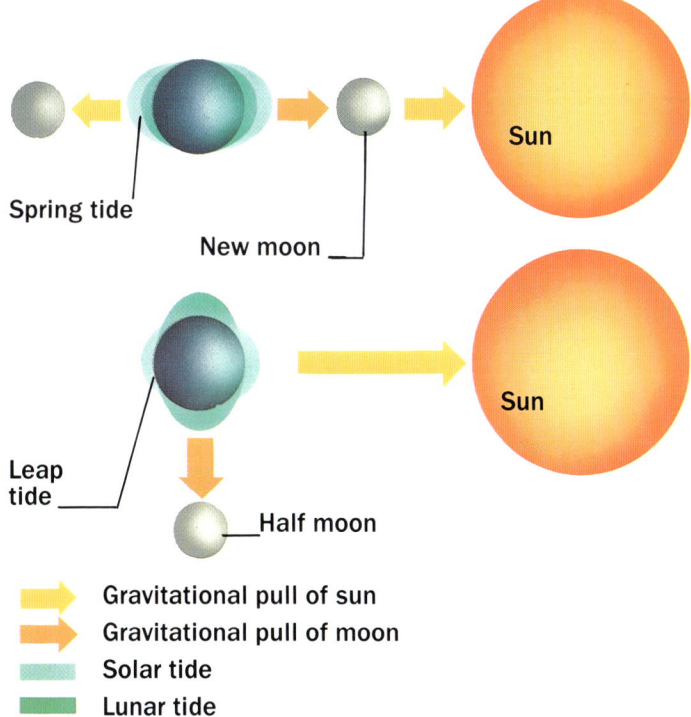

△ Spring tides occur when the moon, sun, and earth are in a straight line and neap tides when they are at right angles.

◁ Tidal waves are caused by underwater earthquakes and get higher toward the shore. They travel very fast and cause severe flooding.

18 OCEAN CURRENTS

Currents in the surface water of the oceans are caused mainly by the prevailing winds, and the rotation of the earth makes the currents move to the right of the wind direction (in the Northern Hemisphere) and to the left (in the Southern). The shapes of landmasses and the ocean bed also affects direction.

CIRCULATION

Currents move in a circular pattern and are called gyres. The gyres rotate in a clockwise direction in the Northern Hemisphere, and in a counterclockwise direction in the Southern Hemisphere.

Ocean currents can be divided into two main types: cold currents and warm currents. At certain times of the year there are also drift currents, such as the Gulf Stream which flows across the Atlantic toward Europe during winter. The overall effect of all these currents is to mix the waters of the earth's oceans.

Another type of mixing occurs when wind blows warm surface water away from a shore. Cooler water from below comes up to take its place in a process called upwelling. The subsurface water often contains nutrients which plantlike organisms feed on. These organisms are then eaten by fish and other sea animals. Such upwelling regions are rich in fish.

→ Cold currents
→ Warm currents
→ Seasonal drift during winter

△ Cold surface currents in the Northern Hemisphere flow generally southward from the North Pole. In the Southern Hemisphere, the cold water circulates around Antarctica.

A thermograph displays different temperatures of the Gulf Stream

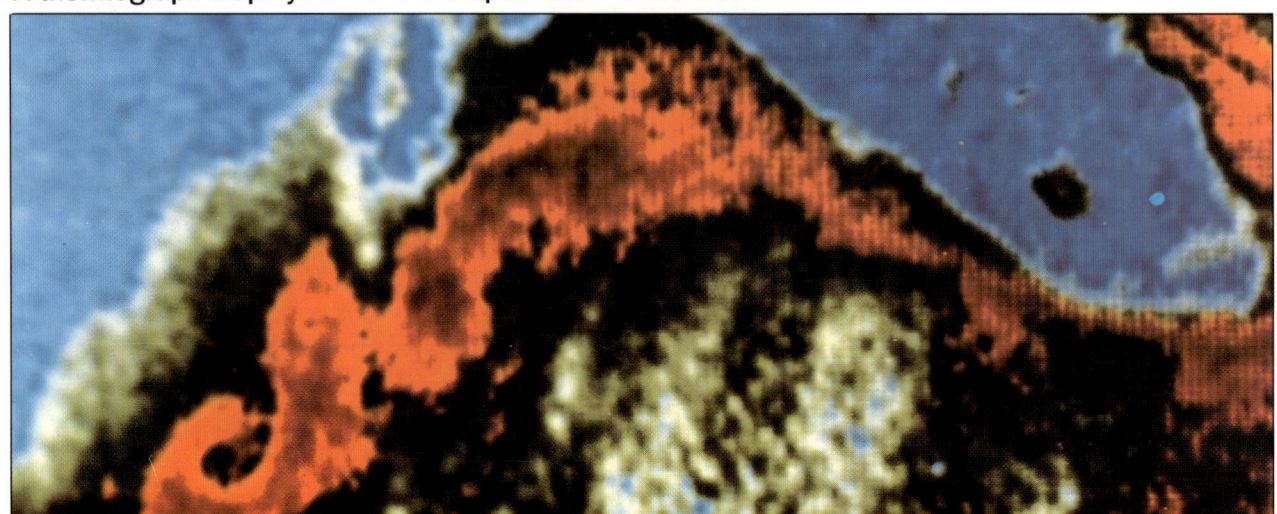

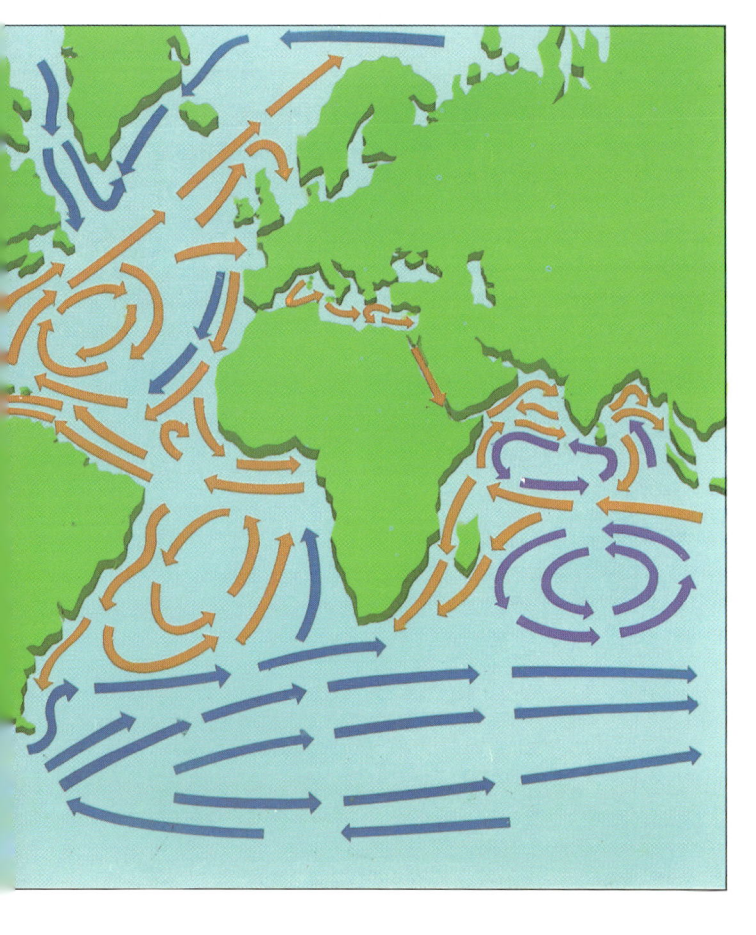

HEAT AND DENSITY

Warm water is less dense than cool water and near the equator, the sun warms the water much faster than at the poles. The salt in ocean water also affects density. As water evaporates from the Mediterranean Sea, it becomes more concentrated in salt, and therefore more dense. Currents of less salty — and less dense — water from the Atlantic Ocean and Black Sea flow in to restore the balance.

The opposite effect takes place in the Baltic Sea of northern Europe. In summer, fresh water from rivers and melting ice flows into the sea and reduces its salinity (and hence density). Then the less dense water at the surface flows southward, forming a current. At the same time an undercurrent of dense, more salty water flows in to take the place of the less dense water.

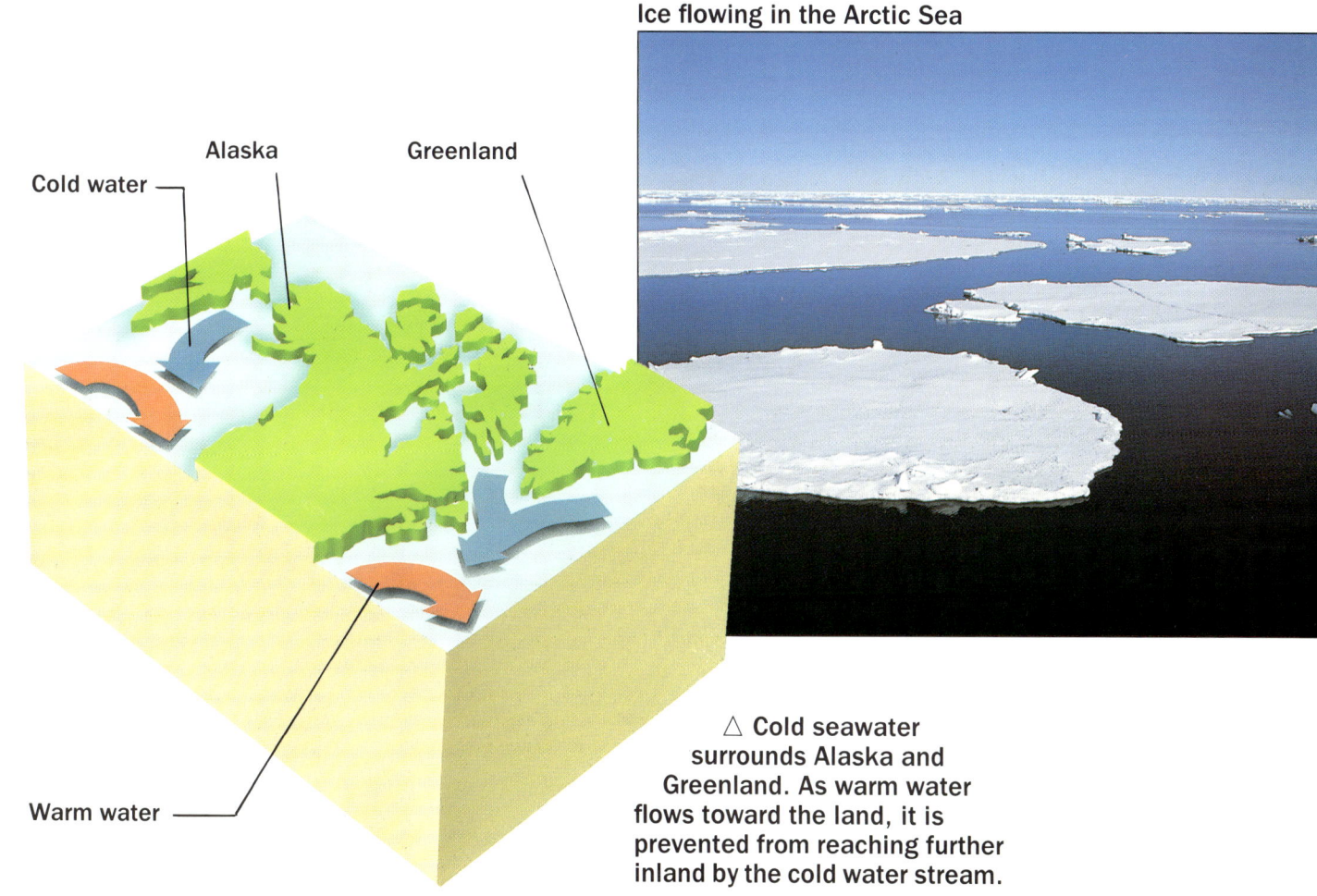

Ice flowing in the Arctic Sea

△ Cold seawater surrounds Alaska and Greenland. As warm water flows toward the land, it is prevented from reaching further inland by the cold water stream.

EXPLORING THE OCEAN FLOOR

Geographers have produced accurate maps of all the world's land surfaces. But over three-quarters of the earth lies underwater, and we know less about it than we do about the surface of the moon. The oceans could provide humankind with food and minerals, and are now being intensely studied by scientists.

MAPPING THE SEABED

Charts of the shallow areas of the ocean have been produced as an aid to navigation for many years. The charts were made using soundings (lowering a weighted rope to measure the depth of the water), and recorded the positions of sandbanks, rocks, and other hazards to shipping. Soundings could only be made far out in the ocean if the piece of rope was long enough. However, real progress was not made until the invention of echo-sounding and the development of manned and unmanned submersibles. Then the science of oceanography really took off.

Some equipment used for deep water exploration (1) Sealink, (2) Perry chamber, (3) Deep-sea camera, (4) Trieste, (5) Box cover, (6) JIM and (7) Tech diver

Echo sounding works by transmitting ultrasonic sound waves to the seabed and measuring the time taken for the reflected waves to return to the surface. From a knowledge of the speed of sound in seawater, the distance traveled by the sound can be calculated (as well as the depth which is half the total distance). Echo-sounding is similar in principle to the sonar used by submarines for detection and navigation.

Early world map

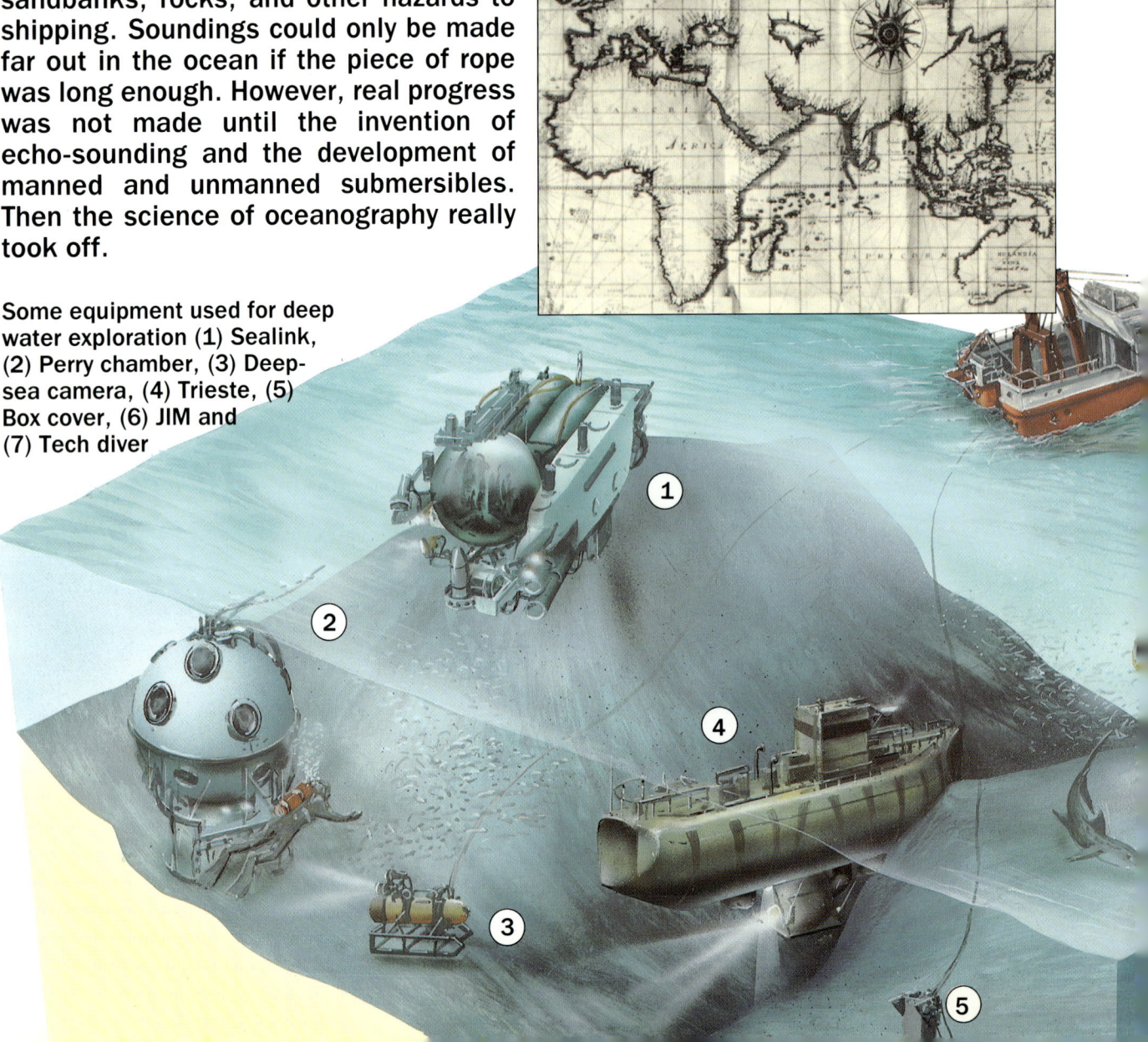

SUBMERSIBLES

Oceanographers use various devices to explore the seabed, but the most versatile — and most expensive — is a manned submersible. It is effectively a small submarine built to withstand the tremendous pressures deep in the ocean. Powered by electric motors, a modern research submersible has a pilot and a crew of up to two observers. It carries lights and cameras — including a television camera to send pictures to the surface — and may have robot "arms" to collect samples from the seabed.

An alternative method of exploration uses a bathyscaphe. This is a strong, pressurized sphere made of steel. It contains various cameras and instruments. In 1960, two scientists in a bathyscaphe descended nearly 36,000 feet to the bottom of the Marianas Trench in the Pacific Ocean.

▷ The modern submersible has come a long way since the first American submarine. It used hand-operated pumps and propellers.

PLUMBING THE DEPTHS

To make a seabed map by taking soundings, put gravel and stones in the bottom of a bowl of water. Put some soil in the water and stir. Using a small weight on the end of a piece of string, measure the depth of water above the various features on the bottom and plot the results on a chart.

MINERAL RICHES OF THE OCEANS

The oceans are a potential source of minerals for mankind — indeed, many of the mineral deposits found on land were formed originally in the sea. Today's oceans get their minerals in two ways: from minerals dissolved in seawater itself, or from deposits located on or under the seabed.

▽ Many mineral deposits are found just offshore. Rivers flowing through rocks rich in ores wash them into the sea. The ores settle in areas and form deposits.

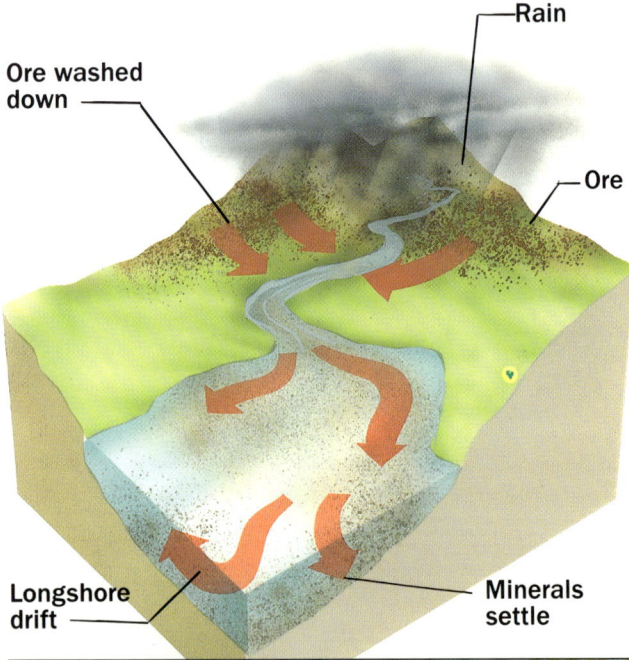

- Ore washed down
- Rain
- Ore
- Longshore drift
- Minerals settle

DEPOSITS

Minerals extracted from the beds of shallow waters, usually along the offshore continental shelf, include metal ores of copper, iron, tin, and titanium. Some metallic gold can also be found. Nonmetallic minerals include phosphates, sulfates, sulfur, shellsand and grit (fine gravel). Rivers that flow through diamond-bearing rocks, such as those off the coast of southwestern Africa, carry alluvial diamonds obtained from the silt and gravel near the river mouths. The minerals are scooped up by dredgers, or pumped ashore along pipes.

Minerals dissolved in seawater are extracted by evaporation — a method used for obtaining salt since ancient times — or by chemical processing. Bromine and iodine, used in medicine and by the photographic industry, are obtained chemically. The chief metal extracted from seawater is magnesium, used for making lightweight alloys.

▽ The map shows the locations of the chief minerals. Manganese is "mined" as nodules off the seabed in deep waters.

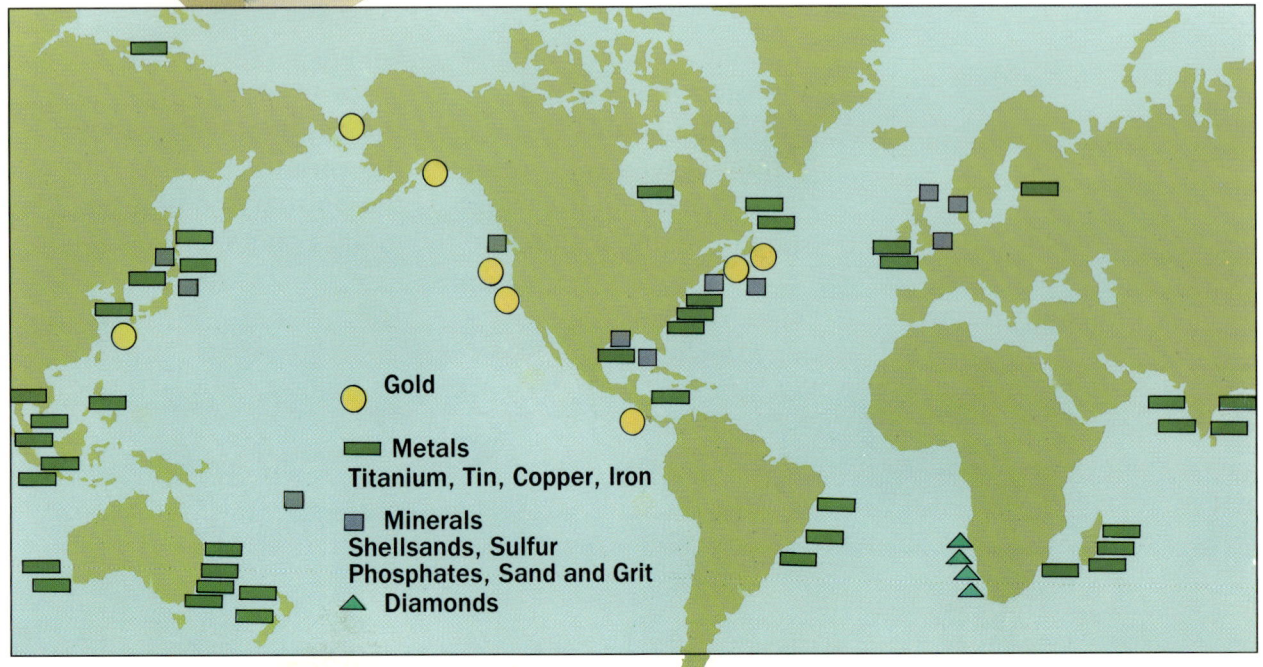

- ● Gold
- ▬ Metals: Titanium, Tin, Copper, Iron
- ▪ Minerals: Shellsands, Sulfur, Phosphates, Sand and Grit
- ▲ Diamonds

EVAPORATION

In hot parts of the world, people extract salt from seawater by running it into shallow "pans" and allowing the heat of the sun to evaporate the water away. You can copy the process by adding salt to a glass or jar of water until no more will dissolve. Pour the salt solution into another glass, and leave it in a warm place, such as near a radiator. As the heat evaporates the water, salt crystals will form.

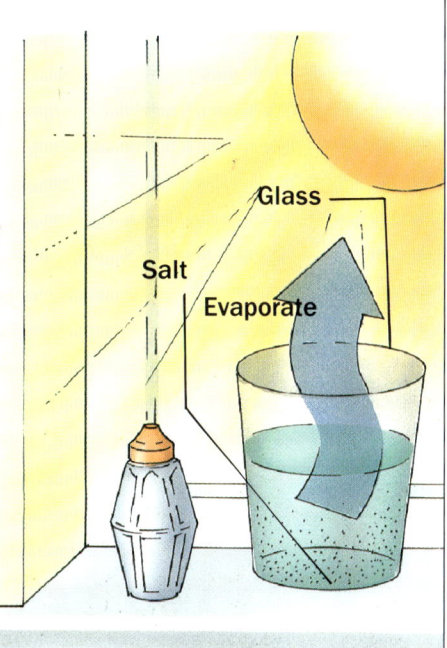

Evaporating seawater for salt

▽ Oil and gas were formed millions of years ago by heat and pressure, as the bodies of millions of small, dead animals and plants were buried at the bottom of the sea.

OIL AND GAS

Some of the most important minerals found under the sea — in fact under the seabed — are oil (petroleum) and natural gas. They are important sources of fuels such as kerosene and gasoline. They also serve as raw materials for various petrochemical products, ranging from drugs and dyes to plastics and explosives.

These so-called fossil fuels were formed millions of years ago from the remains of creatures that lived in the sea. Normally when a plant or animal dies, bacteria make the remains decay, or rot away. But such bacteria need oxygen in order to function, and this was unavailable in the early atmosphere. So the remains fell to the bottom of the sea, where there is little or no oxygen, and different kinds of bacteria worked on them, turning them into hydrocarbons. Layers of clay and silt settled over the hydrocarbons, and pressure and heat converted them into oil and gas. The deposits are "mined" by boring a hole and piping the product ashore.

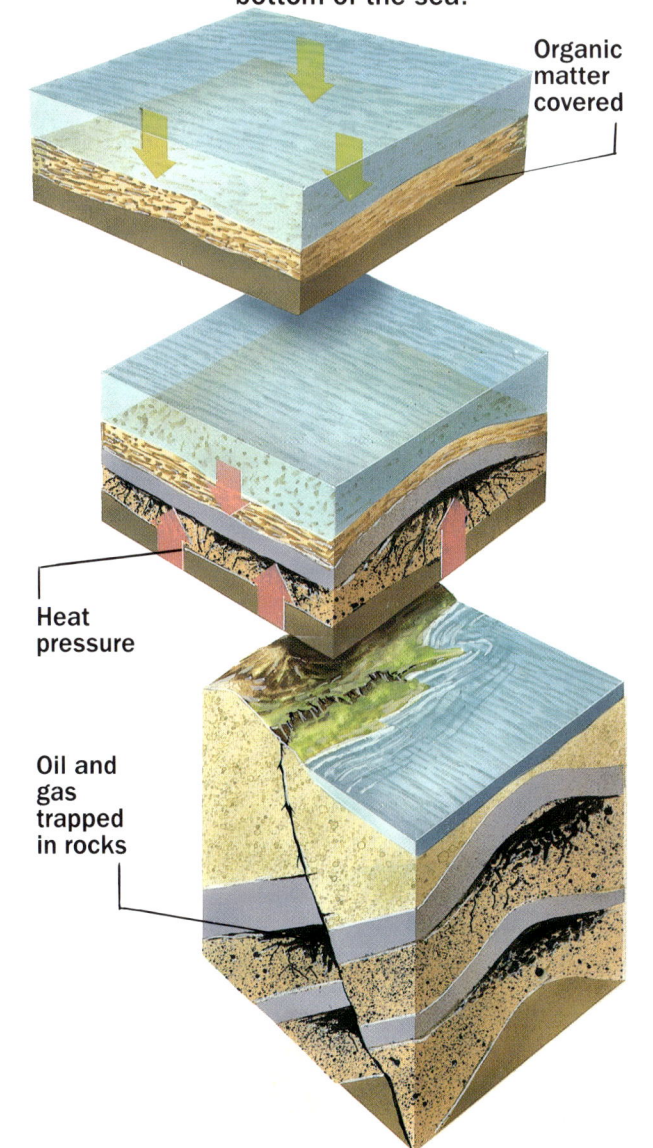

Organic matter covered

Heat pressure

Oil and gas trapped in rocks

24 FOOD FROM THE SEA

Fish are a good source of protein, and for centuries they have been caught and used as food by man and other animals. Today, fish are also processed in factories to make food for pets and farm animals. Mollusks, such as shellfish and crustaceans (crabs, prawns and lobsters), are also caught for food.

OFFSHORE FISHING

Most of the world's major fishing grounds are in shallow waters near the continents. On the continental shelves, the upwelling of nutrients from cooler, deeper water provides a good feeding habitat for the marine population. About 70 percent of all commercial fish are caught in the Northern Hemisphere. For example, herring and cod are netted in the cool Northern Atlantic and sardines in warmer Mediterranean waters. The richest fishing ground in the world lies in the Indian Ocean between Japan and the Philippines.

For a long time, most of the fish caught in the Southern Hemisphere came from the offshore waters of Peru in South America, and the main catch was anchovies. But a new warm sea current disrupted the fishing grounds there.

A modern ocean-going trawler

Fence
Rockwall trap
Fishing rod
Lobster pots
Beach seine

South American fishermen using simple nets

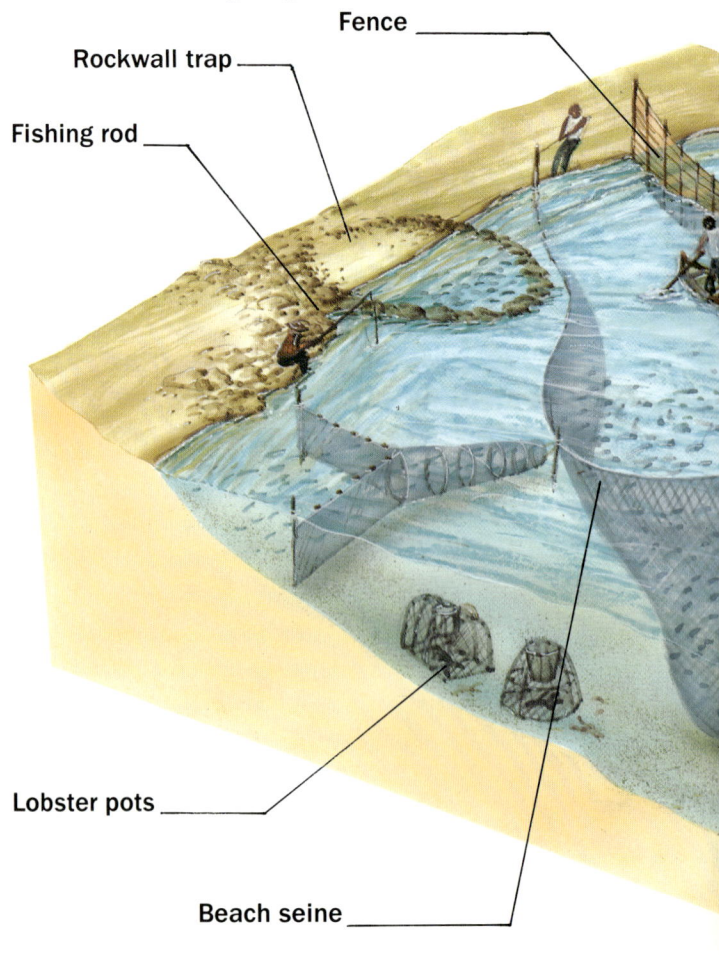

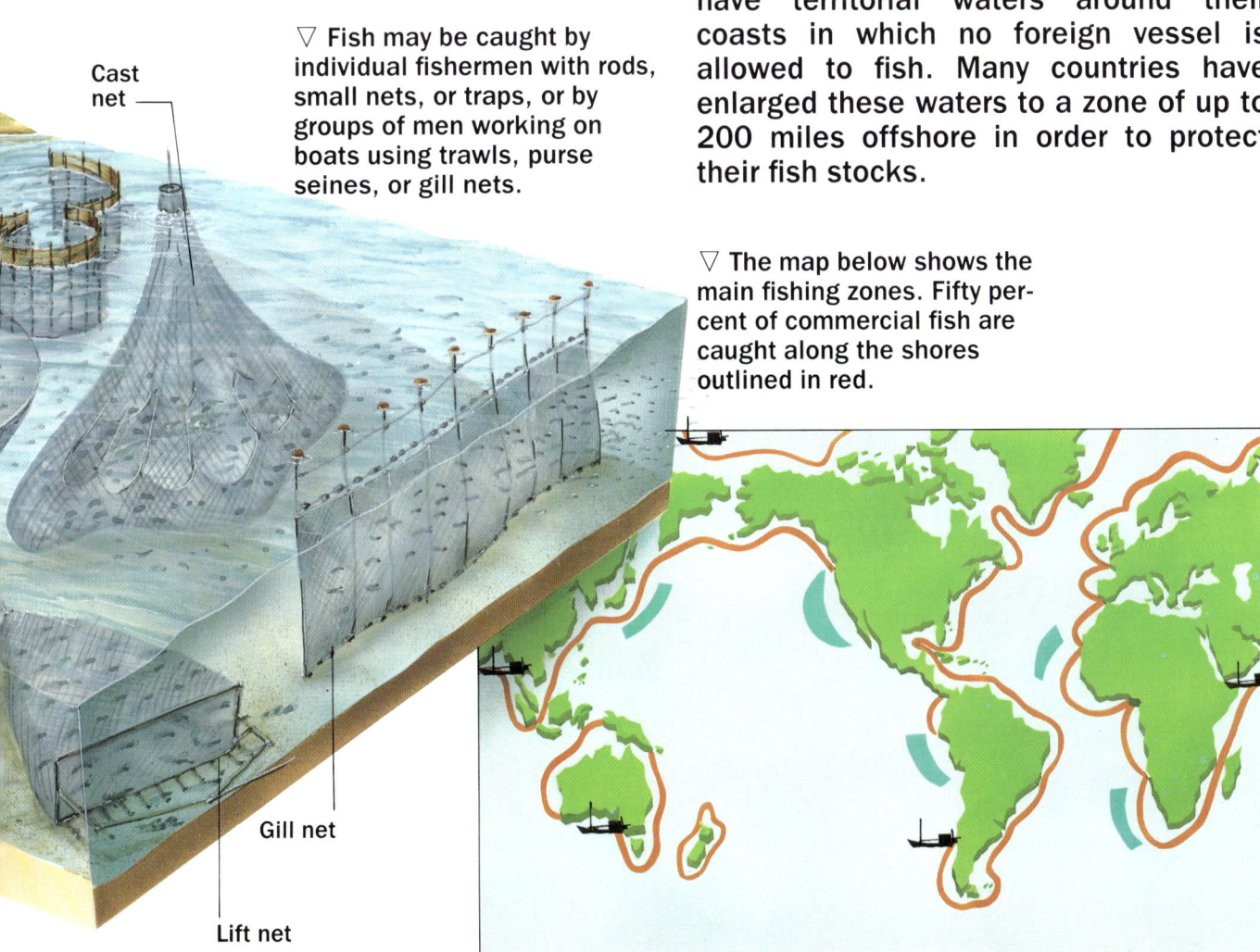

OVERFISHING

Modern fishing vessels are very efficient, and are equipped with a fish-finder (a type of echo sounder to detect shoals of fish underwater) and two-way radios to receive the latest information about the weather and the location of shoals. But the number of fish in the sea is not unlimited, and there is a danger of overfishing. This means that fish will be caught faster than the stocks are being replaced by breeding.

During the late 1980s, commercial fisheries caught almost 90 million tons of fish each year. Experts believe that with effective international control, the annual catch of all fish, crustaceans, and mollusks should never exceed 130 million tons. To enforce this, maritime nations have territorial waters around their coasts in which no foreign vessel is allowed to fish. Many countries have enlarged these waters to a zone of up to 200 miles offshore in order to protect their fish stocks.

▽ Fish may be caught by individual fishermen with rods, small nets, or traps, or by groups of men working on boats using trawls, purse seines, or gill nets.

Cast net
Gill net
Lift net

▽ The map below shows the main fishing zones. Fifty percent of commercial fish are caught along the shores outlined in red.

26 ENERGY FROM THE OCEANS

One of the problems facing the world today is the energy crisis. Fossil fuels (coal, oil, and gas) will not last for ever, and even nuclear power can be hazardous. The constant motion of the tides and waves, and the temperature differences in the oceans, are a vast source of untapped energy.

WATER POWER

Waves have a lot of energy. For example during a storm, waves crashing onto the shore are able to demolish sea walls. But how can this energy be harnessed? Two experiments have been set up which rely on the fact that as a wave passes, the water moves up and down. In one experiment, a long pontoon with a sausage-shaped air bag along its upper surface, is anchored out at sea. As a wave passes by, it compresses the air in the bag. The air then works a turbine that drives an electric generator.

A second type of wave-powered generator consists of a long line of pear-shaped floats. Wave action makes them nod up and down, and this movement is again made to drive an electric generator.

Tides are another source of water power. Slow-speed water turbines are placed in a dam across the mouth of a river. These turn as the tide comes in, and turn again as the tide flows out. The water turbines are used to drive electric generators.

Bay of Fundy, Canada

A Salter's duck at Edinburgh University, Scotland

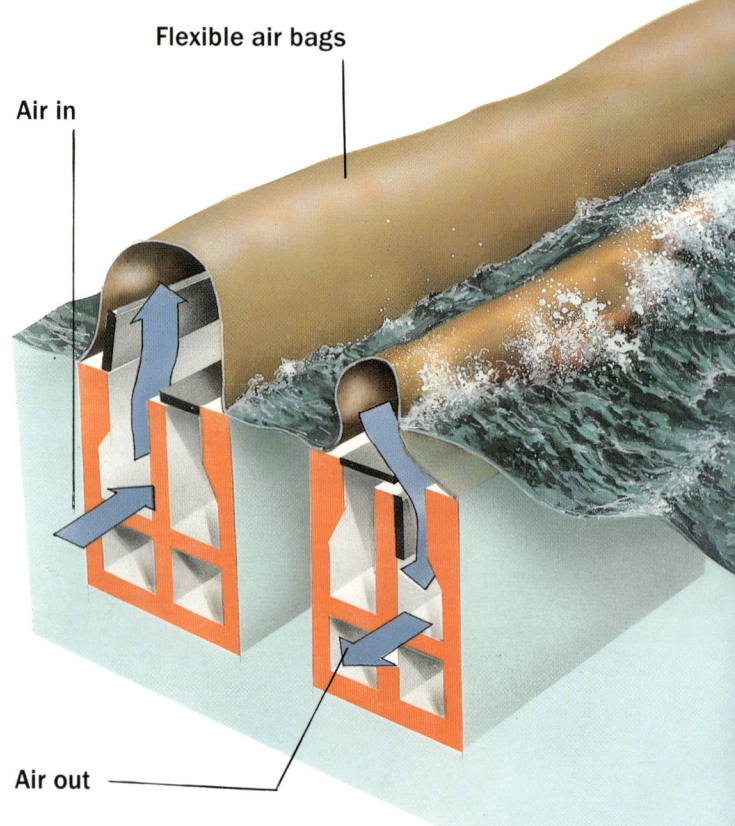

△ Experimental projects have been built which harness the energy produced by waves and tides. Wave-powered electric generators have to be located offshore, where they may be a hazard to shipping. Tidal power plants are built on the shore or at the mouths of rivers.

THERMAL ENERGY

Below the comparatively warm surface waters, the temperature of seawater falls rapidly with increasing depth (see page 13). This temperature difference between surface water and deep water can be used to provide energy. In America, a project has been set up called ocean thermal energy conversion (or OTEC) to do just that.

The project consists of a floating power plant moored in mid-ocean, with a long pipe descending 4,000 feet into the cold water, where the temperature is about 37°F. Pumps lift the cold water up to the power plant where it is used to change ammonia gas into its liquid form. In a heat exchanger, the liquid ammonia is warmed and evaporated back to its gaseous state by warm water from the surface of the sea. The ammonia gas then goes through the same cycle as before. As the liquid ammonia flows around the system, it drives a turbine which generates electricity.

A wave energy machine in Scotland

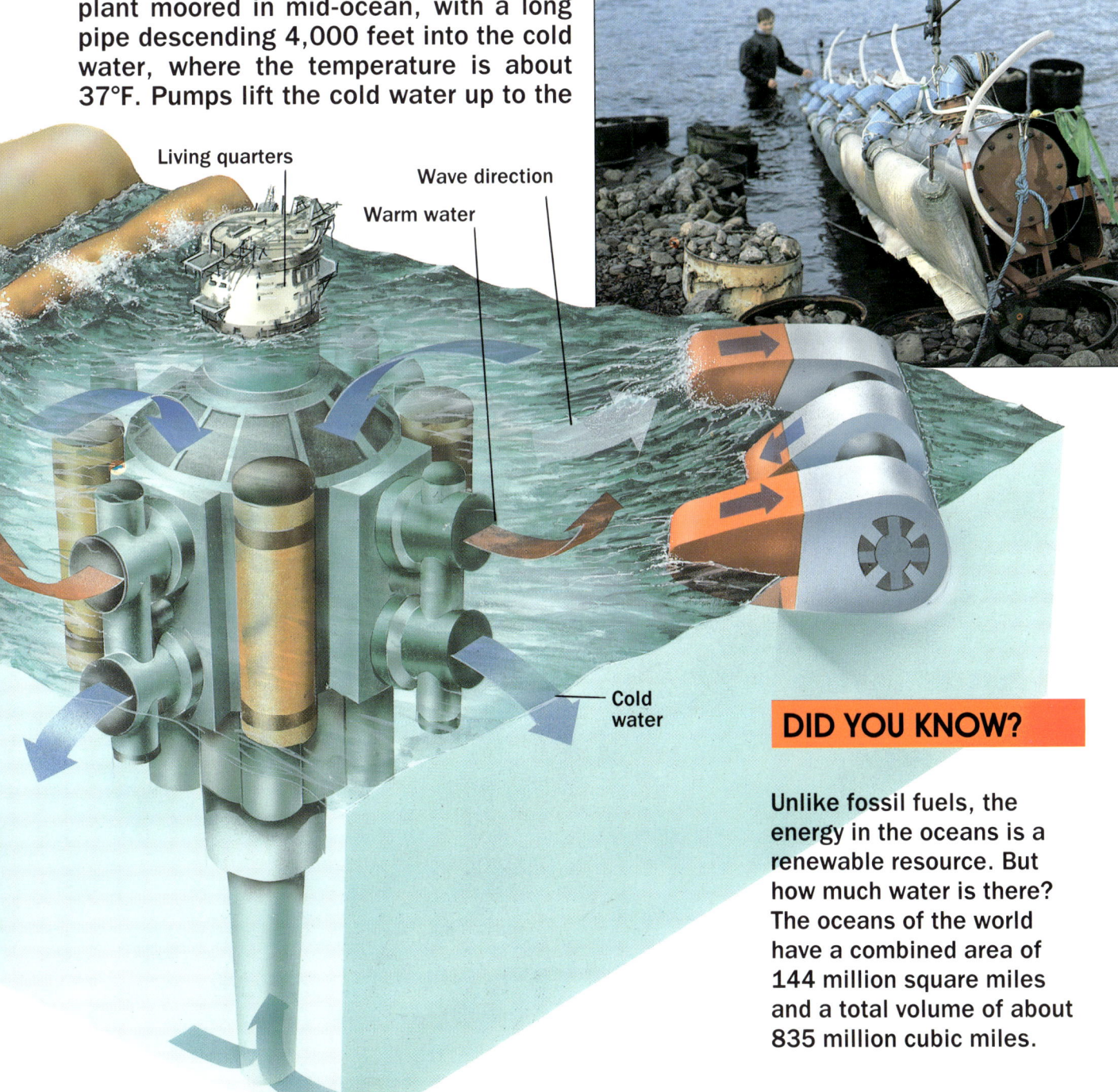

Living quarters
Wave direction
Warm water
Cold water

DID YOU KNOW?

Unlike fossil fuels, the energy in the oceans is a renewable resource. But how much water is there? The oceans of the world have a combined area of 144 million square miles and a total volume of about 835 million cubic miles.

28 THREATS TO THE OCEANS

Because the oceans are so vast, for years, people have been using them as a dumping ground for garbage, sewage and industrial wastes. Accidental spillages of oil have also added to the pollution. But the long-term effects on wildlife – particularly fish – could have disastrous results for humankind.

THE CHANGING OCEAN

Some of man's activities have an indirect effect on the oceans. Atmospheric pollution and increasing levels of carbon dioxide in the atmosphere (from burning forests and fossil fuels) give rise to the greenhouse effect. This, in turn, can lead to global warming – an overall increase in average temperatures throughout the world. One result of this warming could be melting of the ice at the poles. The salinity of the oceans would then change and sea levels would rise, flooding huge areas of land.

Dumping of sewage in the sea alters the amount of oxygen and nutrients in the water. Plankton may thrive for a while, but the phytoplankton – the tiny plants that are the ultimate source of food for sea creatures – would die off. This could lead to a mass reduction in marine life.

Plankton blooms off the New Zealand coast

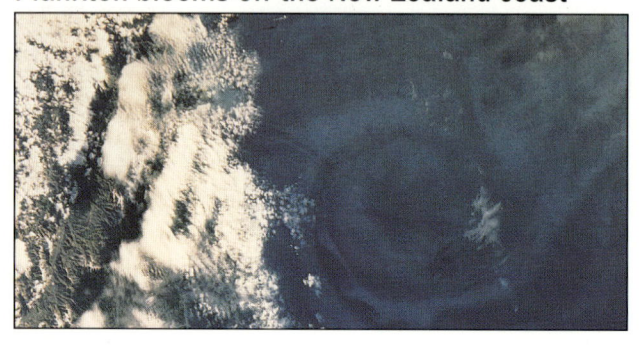

▷ At the end of the last Ice Age the huge ice cap over Scandinavia began to melt. The vast amount of melting water led to a rise in sea levels and later to the formation of the Baltic ice lake.

— Baltic lake
☐ Receding ice cap
▨ Changing coastline

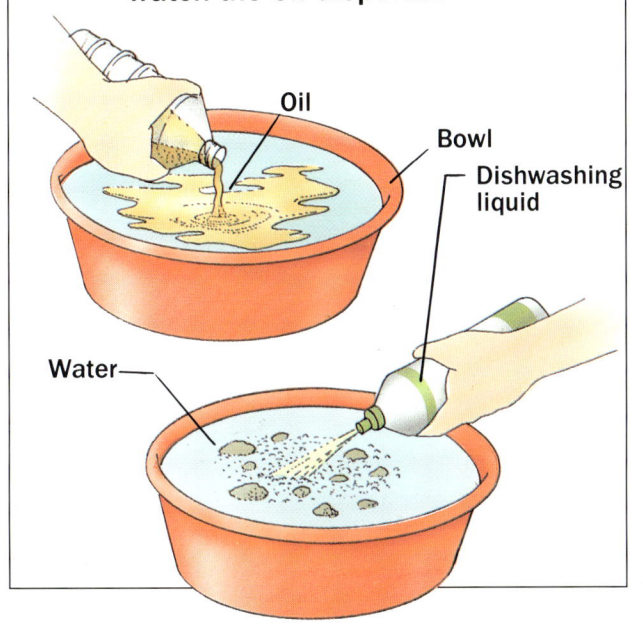

OIL AND CHEMICALS

Crude oil, either spilled accidentally from ships or dumped deliberately from tankers, is a major threat to the oceans. Spilled oil drifts ashore and ends up coating beaches with a black, sticky mess. It gets into the feathers of seabirds, poisoning them as they try to clean their plumage. Scientists have devised various methods to deal with spillages, but the best approach is to prevent them happening in the first place.

Even more dangerous are the toxic chemicals dumped deliberately into the sea, particularly heavy metals such as cadmium, lead, and mercury. During the 1950s and 1960s, Japanese chemical industries dumped 600 tons of mercury compounds into Minamata Bay. The chemicals accumulated in fish which were eaten by the local people. Many people became ill and died, and babies were born deformed. This should serve as a sufficient warning, and bring about an international ban on the dumping of any chemicals in the sea.

Cleaning up oil along the coast

PROJECT

One method of dealing with oil spillages is by using detergents. To see how it works, pour a little oil onto some water. Add some dishwashing liquid, agitate the water, and watch the oil disperse.

Industrial waste being poured into a river

EARLY BELIEFS

Much remains to be discovered about the oceans. Hundreds of years ago, hardly anything at all was known, and people believed that the earth was a large, flat island in the middle of a sea with no boundaries. People also thought that the sea was home to various kinds of terrible monsters.

An old map, with a flat earth and monsters

One early belief was the existence of a sea serpent, many feet long. It was supposed to attack ships and devour sailors. The giant squid was also a myth, until dead squids were discovered. We now know that giant squids can grow up to 60 feet long, and propel themselves through the water at 30 miles per hour. A giant squid has two long tentacles and eight shorter ones. People think that it was the huge tentacles that gave rise to the sea serpent myth.

A less fearsome myth concerns the mermaid. Half woman and half fish, it resembles several others from Greek mythology. Mermaids were supposed to sing alluring songs and tempt sailors to their deaths by drowning. Again, an actual creature may have given rise to this myth. The dugong, or sea cow, is a large, plant-eating mammal that lives in the shallow waters off the coasts of Africa, Asia, and Australia. It has smooth skin and the females have small breasts, which are thought to resemble those of a woman.

The Kraken is a Norwegian sea monster

In Greek mythology, the monsters of the deep were supposed to be under the control of the god of the sea, called Poseidon, the brother of Zeus. People believed the monsters were offspring of gods and mortals. Poseidon's counterpart in Roman mythology was Neptune, usually depicted holding a trident and keeping company with dolphins. He is sometimes shown with a man's upper body and a fish's tail, rather like a male mermaid. Dolphins were themselves thought to be derived from men. We now know that after humans, dolphins are the most intelligent mammals.

Mermaids lured sailors to their deaths

GLOSSARY

Bathypelagic zone
The lowest layer of water in the oceans, with a depth of over 6,000 feet.

Bathyscaphe
A pressurized steel ball in which a person is lowered into the deep ocean.

Cartilaginous
Describing something made of cartilage (gristle), like the skeletons of sharks and related fish.

Continental shelf
The gently sloping seabed close to the shore of a large land mass, where the sea is shallow.

Euphotic zone
The uppermost layer of water in the oceans, from the surface down to about 500 feet.

Greenhouse effect
Overheating of the earth's atmosphere caused by a buildup of gases such as carbon dioxide (which prevents heat from escaping into outer space).

Global warming
Gradual increase in the average temperatures throughout the world, possibly as a result of the greenhouse effect.

Guyot
A flat-topped underwater mountain formed from an eroded underwater volcano; also called a seamount.

Hydrocarbon
A chemical compound of hydrogen and carbon; oil (gasoline) and natural gas are hydrocarbons.

Krill
Microscopic shrimplike animals that live on plankton and provide food for fish and other marine animals.

Mesopelagic zone
The middle layer of ocean water extending from a depth of about 450 feet to 6,000 feet.

Neap tide
A low tide that occurs when the moon and sun are at right angles to each other, and their combined gravity pulls on ocean waters.

Phytoplankton
Microscopic plants that form part of plankton.

Plankton
Microscopic organisms that live in or near the surface of the sea.

Salinity
A measure of the saltiness of seawater.

Spring tide
A particularly high tide that occurs when the moon and sun are in line, and their gravitational pull acts on the waters in the oceans.

Submersible
A small submarine used for exploring the sea.

Swim bladder
A sac inside the body of a bony fish used to control buoyancy.

Water cycle
The process by which water circulates on earth. The sun's heat causes water to evaporate from the surface of the sea as water vapor. This rises into the atmosphere, forming clouds as it cools. Over land, clouds release rain which runs into rivers, finally flowing back to the sea.

INDEX

A
Atlantic Ocean 7, 14, 19
atolls 15

B
Baltic Sea 7, 19
bathypelagic zone 12, 13, 31
bathyscaphes 21, 31
Black Sea 19

C
cartilaginous fish 9, 31
Caspian Sea 11
continental shelves 10, 22, 24, 31
coral reefs 14, 15
crustaceans 10, 11, 24
crustal plates 12, 14
currents 5, 12, 16, 18, 19

D
Dead Sea 11
deep sea life 13

E
echo-sounding 20
euphotic zone 10, 31
evolution of marine life 8

F
fish 8-9, 11, 13, 18
fishing industry 24-5
fishing zones 25
fossil fuels 23, 26, 28

G
global warming 28, 31
Great Barrier Reef 15
greenhouse effect 28, 31
Gulf Stream 18
guyots 14, 31
gyres 18, 31

H
Hawaii 14
hydrocarbons 23, 31

I
islands 14, 15

J
jellyfish 10

K
krill 10, 31

M
mapping the seabed 20
mesopelagic zone 12, 31
mid-ocean ridges 14
minerals 7, 22-3
mountains 5, 12, 14
myths of the ocean 30

N
neap tides 17, 31

O
ocean plain 12
ocean trenches 5, 12, 13
oceanography 20
oil and chemical spillages 29
oil and gas deposits 23
origin of the ocean 6
overfishing 25
oxygen 7, 8, 9, 23, 28

P
Pacific Ocean 5, 7, 12
photic zone 13
phytoplankton 10, 28, 31
placoderms 8
plankton 11, 28, 31
pollution 5, 28-9

R
Red Sea 7

S
salt extraction 22, 23
seabed 5, 14, 20, 21
seafloor spreading 14
spring tides 17, 31
submersibles 20, 21, 31
swim bladders 9, 31

T
thermal energy 27
tidal power stations 26
tides 5, 16, 17, 26

U
upwelling 18, 24

V
volcanic activity 5, 6, 14
volume of the oceans 27

W
water cycle 7, 31
water density 19
water power 26
waves 14, 16, 26

Z
zooplankton 10

Photographic Credits:
Cover and pages 15, 16, 24 bottom, 26 top and 29 bottom: Spectrum Colour Library; page 5: Eye Ubiquitous; pages 7, 12, 17, 19, 23, 26 bottom, 27 and 28: Science Photo Library; pages 8, 13 and 29 top: Frank Spooner Pictures; page 11 top and bottom: NHPA; page 14: J. Allan Cash Photo Library; page 18: National Maritime Museum Picture Library; page 20: Topham Picture Source; pages 21 and 24-25: Bruce Coleman Limited; page 30 top left: The Hulton Picture Company; page 30 top right and bottom: Mary Evans Picture Library.

CROSSAN SCHOOL LIBRARY